SAY WHAT?

THE FASCINATING ORIGINS OF

350+
EVERYDAY
EXPRESSIONS

BY
BEN DOUGLAS

TABLE OF CONTENTS

INTRODUCTION

"It's raining cats and dogs," my grandmother would say as she peered through her kitchen window at the downpour outside. As a child, I'd rush to the glass, pressing my nose against it, desperately hoping to catch a glimpse of a falling feline or a descending dog. Of course, none ever appeared— much to my disappointment.

That's the peculiar magic of idioms: they rarely mean what they say, yet they say exactly what we mean.

You're holding this book because, like me, you're fascinated by these quirky linguistic hand-me-downs that we've inherited from generations past. Perhaps you've wondered why we **kick the bucket** when we die, or why on earth someone would **beat around the bush, pull someone's leg,** or have **ants in their pants**—a condition that, if literal, would warrant immediate medical attention.

These colorful expressions are the spice rack of our language. They're the linguistic equivalent of your grandmother's secret recipe—passed down through generations, modified slightly with each telling, but always retaining their essential flavor. They transform our plain-vanilla statements into memorable declarations, adding just the right dash of imagery and wit to our daily discourse.

But idioms are more than just linguistic garnish. They're time capsules, preserving fragments of history, culture, and human experience within their often puzzling phrases.

When we **spill the beans,** we're tapping into an ancient Greek voting method that could reveal secrets with a single misplaced bean. When we **fly off the handle,** we're reliving the days when poorly made axe heads had a habit of detaching mid-swing.

When we give someone the cold shoulder, we're harking back to medieval feasts where an unwelcome guest might be served the least desirable cut of meat.

And when we **break a leg,** we're carrying forward a theatrical tradition that would make Shakespeare himself raise an eyebrow.

In this book, we'll embark on a journey through fifteen fascinating categories of human experience, each filled with expressions that have stood the test of time.

We'll explore how these phrases were born, why they've survived, and what they reveal about the way our ancestors viewed the world.

From the battlefields that gave us **bite the bullet** to the sailing ships that taught us to **know the ropes,** each chapter unravels the fascinating stories behind the expressions we use every day without a second thought.

You'll discover how ancient myths continue to color our speech, why matters of the heart so often involve sleeves and feet, and what the weather has to do with friendship. We'll delve into the curious connection between money and body parts, explore why death inspires such creative euphemisms, and learn how the animal kingdom became our go-to source for describing human behavior.

So, whether you're a word enthusiast, a history buff, or simply someone who's ever wondered why we don't actually **throw babies out with bathwater**, this book is your ticket to understanding the remarkable stories behind our most colorful turns of phrase.

Let's pull back the curtain on these linguistic treasures and discover why, even in an age of emojis and abbreviated text speak, these ancient expressions continue to **hit the nail right on the head.**

After all, when it comes to understanding idioms, it's **better late than never.**

Now, shall we **get down to brass tacks?**

Ben Douglas

LOVE & RELATIONSHIPS

Puppy love - Temporary romantic feelings typically experienced by young people

Origin: The term "puppy love" emerged from observing how puppies show boundless, indiscriminate affection – much like young people experiencing their first romantic feelings. While Shakespeare used "calf-love" similarly in Twelfth Night (1601), "puppy love" became more popular during the Victorian era as pet ownership grew among the middle class. The concept captures the essence of youthful infatuation through its comparison to a puppy's enthusiastic devotion.

Tie the knot - To get married

Origin: This phrase dates back to the ancient Celtic hand-fasting ceremony, documented as early as 7000 BCE. During these ceremonies, couples would have their hands bound together with cloth to symbolize their union, a practice that continued through medieval times. The ritual was particularly prominent in Scottish culture, where the binding cloth was often the clan tartan. The ceremony lasted exactly one year and one day before the couple decided to make their union permanent.

Match made in heaven - A perfect romantic pairing
Origin: The concept originates from ancient astrological beliefs about divine matrimonial arrangements, particularly in Vedic astrology (c. 1500 BCE). The specific English phrase emerged during the Renaissance period, reflecting the Christian belief that marriages were arranged by God in heaven. The earliest written record appears in the 1650s in Christian theological texts discussing predestination.

Love at first sight - Immediate romantic attraction upon first seeing someone
Origin: The concept dates back to ancient Greek literature, but the exact phrase emerged in the 13th century through courtly love literature. The earliest known English usage appears in Christopher Marlowe's "Hero and Leander" (1598). The phrase gained particular prominence during the medieval period of courtly love, where knights would pledge undying devotion to ladies they had only glimpsed from afar.

Head over heels - Completely in love
Origin: Originally phrased as "heels over head" in the 14th century, describing the physical act of tumbling. The first recorded use comes from Herbert Lawrence's "Contemplative Man" (1771). The phrase inexplicably reversed to "head over heels" in the late 1800s, despite being less logical and became specifically associated with falling in love during the Victorian romantic period.

Break someone's heart - To cause someone extreme emotional pain through romantic rejection

Origin: The metaphorical connection between the heart and emotional pain dates back to ancient Egyptian medical texts (c. 1550 BCE), which believed the heart was the center of emotions. The specific phrase "break one's heart" first appeared in Old English texts around 1050 CE. Geoffrey Chaucer popularized its romantic context in "Troilus and Criseyde" (1374).

Two peas in a pod - Two people who are very similar or close

Origin: This simile emerged in the 16th century when peas became a common crop in England. The earliest printed record appears in John Lyly's "Euphues and His England" (1580). The phrase reflects the observation that peas in the same pod are virtually identical, and it became a popular metaphor for romantic couples during the Victorian era when elaborate botanical metaphors were fashionable.

Cold feet - Nervousness or second thoughts about marriage

Origin: The concept was first documented in Stephen Crane's Maggie: A Girl of the Streets (1893), though it existed earlier. The phrase likely originated from soldiers experiencing literal cold feet before battle, which caused them to lose their nerves. By the early 1900s, it had become specifically associated with pre-wedding jitters, particularly during the Victorian era, when formal weddings became more common.

Blind date - A romantic meeting between two strangers arranged by others

Origin: The term emerged in the 1920s during the rise of American dating culture. First documented in campus newspapers of the era, it reflected the new social freedom of the Jazz Age. The practice became particularly popular during World War II when social organizations arranged dates between servicemen and local women.

Love is blind - Love causes one to overlook faults in the beloved
Origin: This concept dates back to ancient Greek literature, but the exact phrase was first recorded in Chaucer's "The Merchant's Tale" (c. 1395). Shakespeare later popularized it in several works, including "The Merchant of Venice" (1596). The phrase gained particular resonance during the Renaissance when arranged marriages were common, and the tension between love and practicality was a frequent theme in literature.

On the rocks - A relationship in serious trouble
Origin: This phrase originated from maritime terminology in the 1830s, referring to ships damaged by hitting rocks. Its metaphorical application to relationships first appeared in American newspapers in the 1940s. The phrase gained particular prominence during the post-war period, when divorce rates increased and societal discussions about troubled marriages became more open.

Better half - One's spouse or romantic partner
Origin: First recorded in Sir Philip Sidney's Arcadia (1580), the phrase reflects the Platonic concept that humans were originally created as complete beings and later split in two. The term gained popularity in the 17th century, when marriage was increasingly viewed as a partnership rather than a hierarchy. Sir Thomas Browne's Religio Medici (1642) helped popularize the phrase.

Lovebirds - A couple obviously in love
Origin: The term derives from the African parrots of the genus Agapornis, first documented by European naturalists in the 1600s. These birds' tendency to sit closely together in pairs led to the metaphorical use in the 1800s. The phrase became particularly popular in Victorian times when keeping exotic birds as pets was fashionable among the upper classes.

Third wheel - An unwanted person in a social situation, especially when two others are a couple
Origin: This phrase originated in the 1920s as "fifth wheel," referencing the spare tire that became standard equipment in automobiles of that era. The earlier version dates to the 1800s and horse-drawn carriages, where a fifth wheel was the extra steering mechanism that allowed the front axle to pivot. The modern "third wheel" variant emerged in the 1950s among American youth culture, possibly influenced by the growing popularity of motorcycle sidecars, where a third wheel was quite literally an addition to what was designed as a two-person vehicle.

Empty nest - The situation of parents when their children have grown up and left home
Origin: The term emerged in 1950s post-war America, coinciding with psychologists' first scientific studies of "empty nest syndrome." Dr. Pauline Bart's groundbreaking 1971 research paper "Depression in Middle-Aged Women" helped popularize both the phrase and concept. The metaphor draws from nature, where birds' nests become empty as fledglings mature and depart. However, it gained particular resonance during the Baby Boom era, when the pattern of children leaving home became more uniformly timed with college attendance.

Fall out of love - To gradually stop feeling romantic love for someone

Origin: This phrase first gained prominence in the late Victorian era (1870s-1880s), when romantic literature and the concept of "companionate marriage," based on love rather than arrangement, were rising. It appeared in numerous advice columns and etiquette books of the period, reflecting changing social attitudes about marriage and divorce. The novelist George Meredith used it prominently in his 1885 work Diana of the Crossways, helping to popularize the expression as a genteel way to describe the end of romantic feelings.

Ghost someone - To abruptly cut off all communication with someone without explanation

Origin: This term emerged around 2014, first appearing in popular dating blogs and social media posts discussing online dating behaviors. The phrase gained mainstream recognition when the New York Times published an article titled "Ghosting: The Ultimate Silent Treatment" in 2015. The metaphor draws from the supernatural concept of ghosts vanishing into thin air, applied to the sudden disappearance made possible by digital communication platforms.

Swipe right - To indicate interest in someone, derived from the gesture used on dating apps

Origin: The phrase entered popular culture in 2012 with the launch of the dating app Tinder, which pioneered the swipe-based interface for user matching. The gesture was inspired by iPhone designer Jony Ive's natural interface designs and the success of apps like Clear, which used swipe gestures for task management. Within two years, the phrase had transcended its digital origins to become a general metaphor for approval or acceptance in various contexts.

Lovey-dovey - Displaying excessive or schmaltzy affection, marked by demonstrative love and tenderness

Origin: This affectionate term first appeared in print around 1819 in John Poole's comic sketch "Hamlet Travestie." The phrase combines a diminutive form of "love" with "dove," which has symbolized peace and devotion since ancient times, particularly in Middle Eastern and Mediterranean cultures. Its repeated use in Victorian literature, especially in satirical works mocking romantic sensibilities, helped cement its place in common usage. The term gained additional popularity during the sentimental Victorian era when displays of affection became more socially acceptable in public discourse.

Kissing cousins - People or things that are closely related or very similar

Origin: The term emerged in the American South during the early 1800s, where it originally referred to first cousins who were close enough to be permitted to kiss in greeting without scandal. The phrase first appeared in print in 1838 in Caroline Gilman's "Recollections of a Southern Matron," describing acceptable social interactions within extended families. By the 1900s, it had evolved beyond its literal meaning to describe any people or things sharing close similarities or common origins.

Ball and chain - A burdensome constraint or responsibility, often referring to a spouse in a humorous or negative sense.

Origin: The phrase originates from the practice of chaining prisoners by the ankle to a heavy iron ball to prevent escape, a common punishment in the 17th and 18th centuries. The term "ball and chain" was used literally in British and American penal systems. By the mid-19th century, it had evolved into a figurative phrase used to describe a restrictive burden, particularly in marriage, appearing in literature and popular culture to humorously refer to a spouse.

As thick as thieves - Very close or conspiratorial.
Origin: This phrase dates back to at least the 18th century and originally referred to the close-knit relationships among criminals. The word "thick" in this context means intimate or closely allied, and "thieves" were known to operate in secretive, loyal groups. The phrase was popularized in British literature, including Charles Dickens' works, where it described characters who were exceptionally close, often with a hint of secrecy or collusion.

Honeymoon - The initial period of marriage, often characterized by happiness and affection.
Origin: The word "honeymoon" can be traced back to the 16th century and is believed to have Old English and Germanic roots. "Honey" symbolized the sweetness of marriage, while "moon" referred to the fleeting nature of the romantic phase, implying that love, like the phases of the moon, might wane over time. The term appeared in print as early as the 1540s in Richard Huloet's *Abecedarium Anglico Latinum*, and by the 19th century, it became associated with post-wedding vacations.

To butter someone up - To flatter someone excessively in order to gain favor.
Origin: This phrase likely originates from ancient Indian customs, where people would throw balls of butter at statues of the gods as offerings to seek blessings. The practice was rooted in Hindu religious rituals and was meant to curry favor with deities. By the 17th century, the phrase had entered the

English language as a metaphor for excessive flattery, appearing in literary works and common speech.

To bury the hatchet - To make peace or resolve a conflict. **Origin:** This idiom originates from Native American customs, particularly among the Iroquois and other Eastern Woodlands tribes. During peace negotiations, opposing tribes would ceremonially bury weapons, including tomahawks, as a symbolic act of ending hostilities. European settlers recorded this practice as early as the 17th century, and the phrase was later adopted into English, becoming widely used to indicate reconciliation in both personal and political contexts.

COMMUNICATION & LANGUAGE

Beat around the bush - To avoid discussing something directly

Origin: This phrase originated from medieval hunting practices of the 13th century, where paid beaters would literally beat around bushes to flush out game birds. The practice was documented in various medieval hunting manuals. By the 16th century, the phrase had evolved to represent any indirect approach to a subject.

Spill the beans - To reveal a secret or disclose confidential information

Origin: The phrase originates from Ancient Greece's voting system, which existed around 500 BCE. Citizens voted using different-colored beans—white for positive votes and black for negative votes—collected in sealed jars. If someone knocked over the jar, they would "spill the beans" and prematurely reveal the election results. The modern usage first appeared in American magazines in the early 1900s.

Cat got your tongue - Unable to speak or respond.
Origin: This phrase has two potential historical origins. One traces to the English Navy's use of the cat-o'-nine-tails whip, which would render victims speechless with pain. The other connects to Ancient Egypt, where liars' tongues were supposedly cut out and fed to cats. The earliest documented use appears in the mid-1800s, though the practice it refers to may be much older.

Straight from the horse's mouth - Information from the most reliable source
Origin: This phrase originated from horse trading in the early 1900s. A horse's age could be determined by examining its teeth, making this the most reliable way to verify age claims by sellers. The earliest printed reference appears in a 1921 Syracuse Herald newspaper article. The phrase gained popularity during the rise of horse racing and betting in the 1920s, where insider information was highly valued.

Actions speak louder than words - What someone does means more than what they say
Origin: This proverb first appeared in French as "les actions parlent plus fort que les mots" in the works of Michel de Montaigne (1533-1592). The English version emerged in American colonial times, with Abraham Lincoln using it prominently in an 1856 speech. Its first printed appearance in English dates to 1628 in a collection of proverbs by John Pym.

Word of mouth - Information passed from person to person by oral communication
Origin: This phrase dates to the early medieval period when most people were illiterate. Town criers would spread news

"by mouth" rather than written notices, and the phrase appears in Anglo-Saxon chronicles from the 9th century. The term gained renewed importance during the rise of advertising in the early 1900s, when it became recognized as a crucial form of promotion.

Talk the talk - To speak confidently about something, often paired with "walk the walk."
Origin: This phrase emerged from African American jazz culture in the 1940s. Musicians would use "talk" to refer to the distinctive playing style of an instrument and the phrase originally meant to play music in a particular style. By the 1960s, it had spread beyond music into general usage, often paired with "walk the walk" for emphasis on backing up words with actions.

Read between the lines - To discern hidden meaning in communication
Origin: This phrase originated from the practice of writing secret messages between lines of innocent text during the American Revolution. Spies would use invisible ink or code between visible lines of text. The term gained widespread use in the 1840s with the rise of diplomatic correspondence and coded messages.

Put in your two cents - To add one's opinion to a discussion
Origin: This phrase originated from the British "two pennies' worth" and evolved in American usage in the late 1800s. The amount referenced the two-cent stamp cost for sending a letter, suggesting that sharing an opinion was worth at least the price of postage. The phrase appears in print regularly by the 1920s, particularly in newspaper opinion columns.

The walls have ears - Be careful what you say, as others may be listening
Origin: This phrase originated in ancient Persia but gained prominence during the reign of Catherine de Medici in 16th-century France. She had a network of listening tubes installed in the palace walls to spy on courtiers' conversations. Similar systems existed in other European palaces, and the phrase appears in various languages from this period.

Lost in translation - The failure to convey meaning accurately when converting from one language to another
Origin: This phrase gained prominence through the work of Roman translator Marcus Tullius Cicero in the 1st century BCE. In his treatise "De Optimo Genere Oratorum," Cicero discussed the challenges of preserving Greek rhetorical works' meaning when translating to Latin. The modern popularization came from 17th-century Biblical scholars who debated the accuracy of translating ancient Hebrew and Greek texts, particularly during the creation of the King James Bible in 1611. The phrase became firmly established in academic discourse during the 19th-century rise of comparative linguistics.

Through the grapevine - Information spread through informal or unofficial channels
Origin: This phrase originated during the American Civil War, referring to the telegraph lines that were strung between trees, resembling grapevines. The term gained popularity with the 1844 invention of the telegraph and was widely used by the 1850s. The concept was further popularized by the Underground Railroad, which used similar communication networks.

Speak of the devil - Said when a person appears just as they are being discussed
Origin: This is a shortened version of the medieval proverb "Speak of the devil, and he shall appear," which dates back to the 13th century. The original Latin phrase was "mentioned sit diabolus," reflecting the superstitious belief that speaking about the devil would cause him to materialize. By the 16th century, it had evolved into its current form and lost its supernatural connotations.

Have a silver tongue - The ability to speak eloquently and persuasively
Origin: This phrase emerged during the Tudor period in England (1485-1603), when silver was considered the most precious metal for eating utensils due to its alleged ability to detect poison. The association between silver and purity transferred to speech, with the first recorded use appearing in Sir Philip Sidney's "Arcadia" (1580), describing someone whose speech was as pure and valuable as silver.

Chinese whispers - The way information becomes distorted as it passes from person to person
Origin: This phrase originated in the late 18th century, during the period of increased Western trade with China. It first appeared in diplomatic correspondence from British traders who noted the difficulties in communicating through multiple interpreters at Canton trading posts. Originally called "Russian Scandal" in parts of Europe, it gained its current name in British English around 1880. The phrase reflects both the period's communication challenges and problematic colonial attitudes.

Spell it out - To explain something very clearly and in detail, often as if to someone who is slow to understand
Origin: This idiom originated from medieval educational practices in European monasteries. In the 12th century, when literacy was rare, monks taught novices by literally spelling out words letter by letter. The phrase appears in teaching manuals from Canterbury Cathedral's monastery dating to 1225. The modern figurative meaning emerged during the Protestant Reformation, when Martin Luther emphasized the importance of making religious texts accessible to common people.

Off the record - Information given in confidence that should not be officially attributed to the speaker
Origin: This phrase emerged from American journalism practices in the 1920s. The first documented use appeared in a 1926 article in The Syracuse Herald, where it described conversations between reporters and President Calvin Coolidge. The practice became formalized during Franklin D. Roosevelt's presidency, as his press secretary, Stephen Early, established clear guidelines for different types of press interactions. FDR's famous "Fireside Chats" helped establish the contrast between public and private communications.

In black and white - In writing or print, clearly defined and unambiguous
Origin: This phrase dates back to medieval manuscript production in the 13th century when scribes used black ink for the main text and red ink for decorative elements. The first recorded use appears in the 1384 poem "Piers Plowman" by William Langland. The advent of the printing press in the 15th century, which primarily used black ink on white paper,

reinforced the phrase's association with written documentation and clarity of meaning.

Walk the walk - To back up one's talk with actions; to behave in a way that matches one's claims
Origin: This phrase evolved from African American church traditions in the late 19th century. Initially appearing as "walk the walk and talk the talk" in spiritual teachings about living a righteous life, it was documented in several Baptist church newsletters from the 1890s. The phrase gained broader cultural recognition during the Civil Rights Movement of the 1950s and 1960s when leaders emphasized the importance of matching words with actions.

Speak volumes - To convey a lot of meaning without using many words
Origin: This expression originated in 17th-century scholarly circles, first appearing in Francis Bacon's "The Advancement of Learning" (1605). The phrase initially referred to actual volumes of books, suggesting that a single gesture or action could convey as much meaning as multiple books. During the Enlightenment period, it became popular among philosophers and writers who valued concise expression, with Samuel Johnson using it repeatedly in his influential "Lives of the Poets" (1779-1781).

The writing is on the wall - A warning sign that something bad is about to happen.
Origin: This phrase comes from the biblical Book of Daniel, written around the 6th century BCE. In the story, King Belshazzar of Babylon sees a mysterious hand writing on the palace wall during a feast. The prophet Daniel interprets the message as a prediction of the king's downfall, which comes

true that very night. The phrase has since evolved to signify an ominous sign or inevitable misfortune.

Chew the fat - To engage in casual conversation.
Origin: This phrase is believed to have originated from 19th-century sailors who would chew on tough salted pork or fat while chatting during meals. Some scholars trace it back even further to Indigenous North American and European traditions where animal fat was chewed as a social activity. The term became widely popular in English-speaking cultures to refer to friendly, idle chatter.

To read the riot act - To deliver a stern warning or reprimand.
Origin: The phrase originates from the British *Riot Act* of 1714, which allowed authorities to disperse gatherings deemed unlawful. Officials were required to read the act aloud before using force to break up protests or riots. Over time, the phrase shifted from a literal legal order to a metaphor for giving a strong warning or scolding.

Cut to the chase - To get to the point without unnecessary details.
Origin: This idiom comes from the early days of Hollywood filmmaking, particularly silent films of the 1920s. Many movies built up tension with long dialogue scenes before culminating in exciting chase sequences. Writers and directors often advised cutting straight to these action-packed moments, leading to the phrase being used figuratively for skipping unnecessary buildup in conversation or storytelling.

Put a sock in it - A demand to be quiet.
Origin: This phrase likely dates back to the early 20th century, when gramophones had no volume controls. People

would stuff a sock into the horn to muffle the sound. By the 1920s, the phrase had entered common speech as a blunt way to tell someone to be quiet.

Show your true colors - To reveal one's genuine character, often in a negative way.
Origin: This phrase comes from naval warfare in the 17th and 18th centuries when warships often flew false flags to deceive enemies. However, maritime laws required them to hoist their actual national colors before engaging in battle. Over time, the phrase took on a figurative meaning, referring to people revealing their real intentions or nature.

To pull someone's leg - To tease or joke with someone in a playful manner.
Origin: This phrase is believed to have originated in 19th-century England and may have had a darker beginning related to street thieves. Criminals would trip or pull at a victim's leg to distract them while an accomplice picked their pockets. By the early 20th century, the phrase lost its criminal connotation and became associated with lighthearted teasing.

ARTS & ENTERTAINMENT

Stage fright - Nervousness before or during a public performance

Origin: The term first appeared in print in 1876, though the condition has been documented throughout theatrical history. Dr. William Hammond conducted the first medical study of performance anxiety in 1881, describing it in "A Treatise on Nervous Diseases." The phrase gained widespread use during the Victorian era, when public speaking became an important social skill for the middle class.

Break a leg - Good luck (particularly in theater)

Origin: This theatrical saying emerged in the early 20th century and was first documented in print around 1920. The phrase likely originated from Elizabethan theater, where instead of applauding, audiences would bang their chairs on the ground, literally "breaking" the leg of the chair. Another theory connects it to actors having to bow or curtsy (bend their legs) to acknowledge audience appreciation. The superstition against saying "good luck" in theater dates back to 19th-century touring companies.

Waiting in the wings - Ready and waiting for an opportunity to take action

Origin: This phrase derives from the physical "wings" – the offstage areas on either side of the stage – in Restoration-era theaters of the 1660s. These areas became crucial staging spaces after Charles II authorized public theaters to reopen following the Puritan ban. The first written usage appears in theater documentation from the Theatre Royal in 1687, describing actors awaiting their cues in these newly designed stage wings.

Steal the show - To attract the most attention and praise

Origin: This phrase emerged from vaudeville entertainment in the late 1800s. In vaudeville shows, multiple acts would perform in sequence, and occasionally, a lesser-known performer would impress the audience so much that they would overshadow the headlining act. The first printed use of the phrase appeared in theatrical reviews in the 1890s, and it became common in American newspapers by 1910.

Face the music - To confront the consequences of one's actions

Origin: This phrase originated in military circles in the 1830s British Empire. When officers were drummed out of their regiment in disgrace, they had to face the military band playing the "Rogue's March" while being marched out. Some sources also connect it to actors facing the orchestra pit, where the musical conductor sat, during their performances. The first documented use appeared in the New Hampshire Patriot newspaper in 1834.

In the limelight - To be the center of attention or publicity
Origin: The phrase derives from an actual stage lighting technology invented by Thomas Drummond in 1816. Limelight was created by heating calcium oxide (quicklime) to intense temperatures, producing a brilliant white light used to illuminate theater stages throughout the 19th century. The term was first used metaphorically in the 1860s, appearing in Charles Dickens's works. The technology persisted until electric lighting replaced it in the early 1900s.

Swan song - A final performance or piece of work before retirement
Origin: This phrase derives from the ancient Greek belief, recorded by Aristotle in 350 BCE, that swans sing a beautiful song just before death. The theatrical connection emerged in 1790s German opera houses, where retiring singers would perform in Wagner's Lohengrin, which featured the tale of the swan knight. The term gained widespread use after famous soprano Nellie Melba's highly publicized "swan song" performance at Covent Garden in 1926.

Box office - The place where tickets are sold or the commercial success of a performance
Origin: The term originated in 17th-century London theaters, where aristocratic patrons would rent private viewing boxes by leaving payment at a dedicated office. The first documented use appears in Samuel Pepys' diary in 1662, describing the "box keeper's office" at the Theatre Royal. These boxes, which could be booked for entire seasons, became such important revenue sources that the office handling their sales became synonymous with theatrical revenue.

The show must go on - The performance or activity must continue despite difficulties
Origin: This phrase became a theater axiom during the Victorian era (1837-1901) when theaters were businesses that couldn't afford to refund tickets. Circus impresario P.T. Barnum popularized it in the 1870s, who insisted performances continue regardless of conditions. The phrase gained broader cultural significance during World War II when London theaters continued performing during the Blitz.

All the world's a stage - Life is like a theatrical performance where everyone plays various roles
Origin: William Shakespeare immortalized this metaphor in "As You Like It" (1599), though the concept predates him. The Greek philosopher Pythagoras used a similar metaphor in the 6th century BCE. Shakespeare's version appeared in the famous "Seven Ages of Man" speech, which compares life stages to dramatic roles. The phrase became a cornerstone of English literature and philosophy.

Bring down the house - To elicit thunderous applause and approval from an audience
Origin: The phrase emerged from London's theater district in the late 1700s. It refers to the tremendous applause and stomping of feet that would literally shake the building. The first recorded use appears in David Garrick's theatrical memoirs from 1775, describing how certain performances at the Theatre Royal in Drury Lane would cause such audience excitement that the building would tremble.

Prima donna - A temperamental, demanding person who believes they're more important than others

Origin: Originally meaning "first lady" in Italian, this term emerged in Italian opera during the 1720s to designate the leading female singer. The negative connotation developed in the 1800s, as opera stars like Maria Malibran gained tremendous power and made elaborate demands. The first documented use of its modern, pejorative meaning appeared in an 1876 British musical review.

Play to the gallery - To perform in an exaggerated way to please the cheapest seats

Origin: This phrase originated in Elizabethan theater, where the "gallery" referred to the highest, cheapest seats. The first documented use appears in theater critiques from 1836. The term initially described actors who exaggerated their performances so those seated furthest away could appreciate them, but it evolved to suggest pandering to less sophisticated audiences.

Behind the scenes - In private, away from public view, where real work happens

Origin: This theatrical term emerged in the late 1700s, during the rise of elaborate stage machinery and scenery. The first documented use appears in David Garrick's correspondence about London's Drury Lane Theatre in 1767. By the 1820s, the phrase gained broader use beyond theater circles, particularly in political journalism, where it described the hidden workings of government.

Show stopper - A performance or act so impressive it interrupts the show with applause

Origin: This term originated in vaudeville theaters of the 1880s. It literally referred to acts that received such prolonged applause that the show had to stop temporarily. The phrase first appeared in print in Variety magazine in 1908. The concept became especially associated with Broadway musicals in the 1920s and 1930s.

Cat's pajamas - Something or someone extraordinary or excellent

Origin: This phrase emerged in American slang during the Jazz Age of the 1920s. It was coined by cartoonist Thomas A. Dorgan, who is known for creating popular slang terms. The phrase appeared alongside similar "cat" expressions like "cat's whiskers" and "cat's meow" during a period when the word "cat" became associated with jazz musicians and cool characters. Its popularity peaked during the flapper era.

Curtain call - The appearance of performers on stage after a performance to acknowledge applause

Origin: This tradition began in the early 1800s at London's Theatre Royal, Drury Lane. The practice emerged partly as a way for theater managers to prove to skeptical audiences that star actors were really performing and not being substituted by look-alikes. The first documented "recall" was of acclaimed actor Charles Kemble in 1824, and the practice soon became formalized with strict rules about the order of appearance based on role importance.

Green room - A waiting room for performers before going on stage

Origin: This term dates to the 1670s at London's Blackfriars Theatre, where the off-stage waiting area was painted green to help soothe actors' eyes after exposure to the intense lime lights used on stage. Another theory links it to Elizabethan theaters, where actors waited on a patch of grass before entering the stage. The first printed reference appears in

Thomas Shadwell's "A True Widow" (1678), referencing "The Green Room Behind the Scenes."

Upstage - To draw attention away from another performer
Origin: This term emerged from 19th-century theater architecture when stages were built on an incline (or rake) that sloped upward away from the audience. The back of the stage was literally "up," and when an actor moved there, others had to turn their backs to the audience to face them. The practice was first criticized in an 1881 issue of "The Stage" newspaper, which condemned actors who deliberately moved upstage to force their colleagues into disadvantageous positions.

Ham it up - To overact or perform in an exaggerated way
Origin: The term originated in the 1880s American minstrel shows, where performers used ham fat to remove their blackface makeup. Less talented actors spent more time wiping off makeup, extending their stage time, leading to the term "hamfatter" for poor performers. The phrase evolved in vaudeville circuits, with the first printed use of "ham actor" appearing in Variety magazine in 1882 and becoming mainstream theater slang by 1900.

Pull out all the stops - To do everything possible to achieve the best result.
Origin: This phrase comes from the world of pipe organs, where "stops" are the controls that regulate airflow to different sets of pipes. In the 18th and 19th centuries, organists would "pull out all the stops" to allow maximum sound, creating a grand and powerful musical effect. The phrase was first used figuratively in the 19th century to mean making a full effort, appearing in literature such as Matthew Arnold's writings in the late 1800s.

Bells and whistles - Extra features added to something, often unnecessary but designed to impress.

Origin: This phrase originates from the world of mechanical devices, particularly steam engines and early amusement rides, which often featured literal bells and whistles to attract attention. By the late 19th and early 20th centuries, "bells and whistles" became a metaphor for flashy but nonessential additions to products, especially in advertising and sales. The term remains popular in discussions about consumer goods, software, and technology, where additional features are included to enhance appeal.

Bull in a china shop - A person who behaves clumsily or recklessly in a delicate situation.

Origin: This idiom first appeared in English in the early 19th century, though similar imagery can be traced back to earlier European fables. The phrase likely originated as a humorous exaggeration, as bulls are not known to enter china shops. It was popularized in literature and became a standard metaphor for any disruptive or careless individual in fragile circumstances.

Raining cats and dogs - Raining very heavily.

Origin: This phrase has origins in Northern European architecture and Norse mythology. In old Nordic and Germanic houses with thatched roofs, cats and dogs would often nestle into the thatch for warmth. During heavy storms, the animals would either slip or be driven out by the rain. Additionally, Odin, the Norse god of storms, was often pictured with dogs and wolves (representing wind), while witches, who rode through storms, were depicted with black cats.

Barking up the wrong tree - Pursuing a mistaken course of action

Origin: This phrase emerged from American raccoon hunting in the late 1700s. Hunters used dogs to track raccoons at night, following their scent to a tree and barking to signal their quarry's location. The phrase first appeared in print in Davy Crockett's "Narrative of the Life of David Crockett" (1834). Raccoons would often outsmart their pursuers by leaping between trees through connecting branches, leaving the dogs barking at an empty tree.

Bird's eye view - A view from above.

Origin: The concept dates back to 16th-century European mapmakers and military strategists who would climb to high vantage points to sketch landscapes as they might appear to a bird in flight. These early "bird's eye" maps became crucial military tools, with mapmakers studying bird flight patterns to understand perspective and elevation better. The term was first documented in 1599 in John Stow's "Survey of London," where he described viewing the city from church steeples to create accurate maps.

Fish out of water - Someone in an uncomfortably unfamiliar situation.

Origin: This metaphor dates back to medieval monasteries where fish ponds were maintained for Lent. Monks documented the behavior of fish when temporarily removed for sorting or cleaning, noting their obvious distress. The phrase appears in Chaucer's Canterbury Tales (c. 1390) in Middle English, showing its deep roots in the English language. Similar expressions exist in ancient Greek texts, suggesting the metaphor may be even older.

Night owl - Someone who stays up late or is active at night.
Origin: The term evolved from medieval European watchmen who worked the night shift. These guards would observe actual owls during their watches and noted their keen night vision and silent vigilance. By the 1500s, the phrase appeared in various texts describing both nocturnal birds and people who stayed awake at night. Shakespeare used it in "Twelfth Night" (1601), helping to popularize the expression.

Wild goose chase - A futile pursuit or search.
Origin: The term originated in the 16th century as a type of horse race where riders followed a lead horse that would veer off unpredictably in different directions, like a flock of wild geese in flight. Shakespeare immortalized the phrase in "Romeo and Juliet" (1595), where Mercutio describes the chaotic nature of such races. By the late 1600s, the phrase had evolved beyond its equestrian origins to describe any hopeless pursuit.

Lion's share - The largest or best portion.
Origin: This phrase comes from Aesop's fable "The Lion Goes Hunting," written around 600 BCE. In the story, a lion hunts with several other animals but claims all portions of the prey through various justifications: the first portion because he's king, the second for his courage, and so on. The term became particularly popular during the colonial era when it was used to describe how imperial powers divided conquered territories.

Let the cat out of the bag - To reveal a secret unintentionally
Origin: This phrase originated in medieval English marketplaces of the 1500s, where dishonest traders would substitute cats for more valuable piglets in bags sold to unwary customers. The fraud would be revealed when the bag was opened, and the cat escaped. The first printed reference appears in a London newspaper from 1760, warning readers about marketplace scams.

Busy as a bee - Extremely industrious.
Origin: This simile emerged from medieval beekeeping observations in the 13th century. Monastery records show that beekeepers documented a single bee visiting between 2,000 to 5,000 flowers daily, with some colonies containing up to 60,000 bees. The phrase gained prominence during the Industrial Revolution when it was used to promote the virtues of hard work and productivity in Victorian society.

Kill two birds with one stone - Accomplish two objectives with a single action.
Origin: The phrase reflects ancient hunting practices using slings and stones. While the exact origin is unclear, similar expressions appear in ancient Greek and Latin texts. The specific English version gained popularity in the 1600s, with one of its earliest appearances in Gabriel Harvey's works in 1589. The practice of stone-throwing as a hunting method was common among shepherds who needed to protect their flocks while also providing food.

Monkey business - Mischievous or questionable behavior.
Origin: This phrase emerged in the mid-1800s with the rise of organ grinders, who used trained monkeys to collect money. These performers often served as distractions for pickpockets,

leading to the phrase's association with deceptive practices. The earliest printed use appears in Herman Melville's The Confidence-Man (1857), which describes suspicious behavior on a Mississippi riverboat.

Snake in the grass - A deceitful or treacherous person. **Origin**: The Latin poet Virgil first used this phrase (latet anguis in herba) in his Eclogues, written around 42-39 BCE. It reflected the very real danger Roman agricultural workers faced from vipers hiding in tall grass. The phrase entered the English vernacular through translations of classical texts during the Renaissance, with its first recorded English use in 1696 by John Dryden.

A wolf in sheep's clothing - Someone who hides malicious intent behind a harmless facade **Origin**: This phrase comes from the Bible, specifically Matthew 7:15, warning about false prophets. The metaphor was popularized through Aesop's fables in ancient Greece around 600 BCE. The phrase gained widespread use during the Protestant Reformation in the 16th century, when it was used in religious propaganda by both Catholics and Protestants.

Bear the brunt - To endure the worst part of something. **Origin:** The phrase dates back to the 14th century, when the word "brunt" originally meant a violent attack or blow, often used in the context of warfare. Early documented uses appear in Middle English literature, such as in the works of Geoffrey Chaucer. By the 17th century, the phrase evolved into a metaphor for withstanding the main force of any adversity, not just physical attack.

Ants in your pants - To be unable to sit still due to excitement or nervousness.

Origin: This playful idiom likely originated in the early 20th century in the United States. Its vivid imagery evokes the uncomfortable sensation of ants crawling inside clothing, making it an apt metaphor for restlessness. While it does not appear in formal texts from earlier periods, it gained popularity in children's rhymes and informal speech.

Make a mountain out of a molehill - To exaggerate a minor issue into a major problem.

Origin: The phrase has its roots in ancient proverbs, with a similar Latin expression, "Parturient montes, nascetur ridiculus mus" ("The mountain will labor, and a ridiculous mouse will be born"), found in Horace's works around 20 BCE. The English version was first recorded in the mid-16th century by the clergyman Nicholas Udall. Its enduring use reflects the timeless tendency to overreact to trivial matters.

Get someone's goat - To irritate or annoy someone.

Origin: This idiom's origin is debated, but one plausible theory links it to horse racing in the United States in the late 19th century. Goats were often placed with racehorses in stables to calm them, as goats' presence was believed to have a soothing effect. Removing the goat could upset the horse, affecting its performance, hence the metaphor for causing annoyance or agitation.

Can't see the forest for the trees - To be so focused on small details that one misses the larger picture.

Origin: This idiom, which is rooted in European literary traditions, dates back to the 16th century. It first appeared in print in a collection of proverbs by John Heywood in 1546.

The metaphor reflects the human tendency to become overly preoccupied with minor elements while overlooking broader contexts.

Don't look a gift horse in the mouth - To not criticize or question a gift.
Origin: This idiom originates from the practice of examining a horse's teeth to determine its age and value, a method well-known in ancient cultures. The phrase appears in early texts such as the writings of St. Jerome in the 4th century AD, who used it in a letter. By the 16th century, it had become a common proverb in English, emphasizing gratitude over scrutiny.

A different kettle of fish - A completely different matter or situation.
Origin: The phrase dates back to the 18th century in Britain, where aristocrats hosted outdoor gatherings known as "kettle of fish" parties. At these events, fish were boiled in large kettles and eaten fresh. The term came to symbolize a unique or alternative way of doing something, and by the 19th century, "a different kettle of fish" had evolved into a figurative phrase referring to a contrasting or unrelated topic.

A bird in the hand - Having something certain is better than taking a risk for more.
Origin: This phrase traces its roots to medieval falconry, where having a captured bird in hand was more valuable than trying to catch one in the wild. Variations of the saying appear in English proverbs as early as the 15th century, with the full version "A bird in the hand is worth two in the bush" appearing in John Ray's *A Handbook of Proverbs* (1670). The

phrase has remained a cautionary proverb about valuing certainty over uncertain gain.

Badger to death - To harass or pester someone relentlessly.
Origin: This phrase comes from the cruel 18th- and 19th-century sport of badger-baiting, where dogs were set upon a badger in a pit until the animal was exhausted or killed. The term "badgering" became associated with persistent torment, and by the mid-19th century, "badger to death" emerged as a metaphor for relentless nagging or pressure in everyday language.

Till the cows come home - For a very long time, often indefinitely.
Origin: The phrase dates back to at least the 16th century and is rooted in the slow and leisurely habits of cows, which would often graze in fields and return to their barns at their own unhurried pace. The phrase was first recorded in Scottish literature in the early 1600s, emphasizing an indefinite or prolonged period of waiting. Over time, it became a common expression for something that could go on endlessly.

Happy as a clam - Extremely happy and content.
Origin: The full version of this phrase, "happy as a clam at high water," dates back to early 19th-century New England. Clams are most vulnerable when the tide is low, making high water a safe and ideal condition for them. The phrase appeared in print as early as 1833 in American newspapers and was popularized in *The Knickerbocker* magazine in 1848. It remains a widely used idiom for expressing joy and satisfaction.

Asleep at the wheel - Being inattentive to one's responsibilities, especially in a leadership position
Origin: The phrase emerged in the early 1900s with the rise of automobile culture in America. It first appeared in newspaper accident reports around 1904, with the Chicago Tribune being one of the first major papers to use it regularly in their automotive section. The phrase gained broader metaphorical meaning during the 1929 Stock Market Crash when financial leaders were accused of being "asleep at the wheel" as the economy collapsed.

Hit the road - To begin a journey or depart
Origin: This phrase emerged in the early 1900s during America's growing automobile culture. The first documented use appeared in American newspapers around 1908, when motorcars were becoming common on public roads. Initially meaning to physically travel on roads, it evolved into a broader metaphor for departing or starting any kind of journey by the 1920s. The term gained widespread popularity during

the Great Depression when many Americans traveled seeking work.

Off the beaten path - Away from commonly traveled routes; in an unusual location
Origin: This phrase dates back to 16th-century England, first appearing in print in 1570 as "beaten track." The term "beaten" referred to foot traffic wearing down a path through frequent use. Shakespeare used a variation in Henry VI, Part 3 (1592). The phrase gained popularity during the Age of Exploration when European travelers sought routes beyond established trade paths. By the 1800s, it had evolved into a metaphor for unconventional choices.

Make tracks - To leave quickly; to hurry away
Origin: This American phrase originated in the 1830s, likely from Native American tracking terminology. Early frontiersmen and trappers used it to describe leaving visible trails in snow or soft ground. The phrase first appeared in James Fenimore Cooper's frontier novels. By 1850, it had evolved to mean leaving quickly in any context.

Train of thought - A connected sequence of ideas or reasoning
Origin: This phrase originated in the 1650s during the Scientific Revolution, first appearing in Thomas Hobbes's landmark work Leviathan (1651). Hobbes used the metaphor of a train—meaning to draw or drag something—to describe how one thought leads to another in a connected sequence. The concept was heavily influenced by the mechanical philosophy of the era, which viewed the mind as operating according to fixed laws like a machine. It gained popularity as

railways emerged in the 1800s, giving the phrase new resonance.

On the wrong track - Following an incorrect or misguided course of action

Origin: This phrase originated in the 1820s during America's early railroad expansion. Train accidents caused by switches set to the wrong tracks were common dangers in early rail travel. The phrase first appeared in railroad company documents warning workers about track-switching errors. By the 1850s, it had evolved into a general metaphor for misguided decisions, coinciding with the railroad's growing importance in American life.

Miss the boat - To lose an opportunity by being too slow to act

Origin: This idiom emerged in the mid-1900s when steamboat travel was a crucial form of transportation. Missing a scheduled departure could mean waiting days or weeks for the next boat. The phrase first appeared in print in the 1840s in port city newspapers. Originally literal, it became metaphorical during the California Gold Rush when missing a boat could mean missing out on a fortune.

End of the line - The final point or conclusion

Origin: This phrase emerged from railroad terminology in the 1840s, referring to the physical end of a rail line. Early railroad maps and timetables used the term to indicate terminal stations. The phrase gained metaphorical meaning during the rapid expansion of railroads across America, symbolizing finality in any context.

Hit the ground running - To begin an activity with great energy and enthusiasm

Origin: This phrase first appeared in American newspapers of the late 19th century, often in sports and horse racing contexts. The imagery likely came from dismounting horses or vehicles while maintaining forward motion - a common practice in early American rural life. The phrase gained widespread use during World War II through military training terminology, though this wasn't its origin. By the mid-1900s, it had evolved into common business terminology for energetic starts to projects or ventures.

Running on empty - Operating with depleted resources or energy

Origin: This phrase emerged in the 1930s during the Great Depression when running out of gas was a serious concern for motorists. It gained wider popularity after the 1973 oil crisis when fuel shortages became a national concern. The phrase was popularized by Jackson Browne's 1977 song of the same name, reflecting the era's energy consciousness.

Off the rails - To go wrong or become erratic and uncontrolled

Origin: This phrase emerged in the 1850s during the rapid expansion of American and British railways. Early railroad accidents often occurred when trains literally derailed from poorly maintained or improperly laid tracks. The London Times first documented the literal usage in 1852, and by the 1870s, the phrase had evolved into a metaphor for anything going awry. The devastating consequences of actual derailments made this an especially powerful metaphor for Victorian audiences.

Derailed - Disrupted or thrown off course
Origin: This term emerged in the 1850s during the rapid expansion of railroads in Europe and America. It was first used technically in railroad accident reports and engineering documents. The word "derail" was coined by English railway engineers in 1850. By the 1880s, it had evolved into a metaphor for any disrupted plan or process.

Fifth wheel - An unnecessary or unwanted extra person
Origin: This phrase originated from wagon design in the 1800s. The fifth wheel was a spare steering mechanism that could replace a broken one. First documented in carriage-maker's manuals from the 1830s, it evolved into a metaphor for superfluity by the 1900s. The phrase reflected the complex mechanical nature of horse-drawn transport.

Put the cart before the horse - To do things in the wrong order or reverse logical sequence
Origin: This phrase dates back to ancient Greece, appearing in Lucian's works in the 2nd century CE. The Latin version "currus bovem trahit" (the cart draws the ox) was common in medieval European writings. The modern English version first appeared in print in John Heywood's 1546 collection of proverbs, reflecting the agricultural society's understanding of proper working order.

Backseat driver - A passenger who gives unwanted advice to the driver; by extension, anyone who interferes in matters they're not directly responsible for
Origin: This term first appeared in the early 1920s, specifically in a 1921 edition of the Nebraska State Journal. It emerged alongside the rise of closed-body passenger cars, in which the backseat became physically separated from the

driver's seat. The phrase gained popularity during the 1930s as automobiles became more common among middle-class families. It was frequently used in popular magazines like The Saturday Evening Post to describe meddlesome passengers.

Cover a lot of ground - To deal with many topics or accomplish many things
Origin: This phrase emerged from military terminology in the 1700s, referring to troops traversing large areas during campaigns. First documented in British military dispatches around 1750, it reflected the importance of territorial coverage in warfare. By 1800, it had evolved into a metaphor for accomplishing multiple tasks.

Get the show on the road - To begin an activity or journey; to start something moving
Origin: This idiom originated in the world of traveling circuses and vaudeville shows in the late 1800s. It was first documented in circus manager records around 1870, referring to the literal act of moving a show from one town to another. The Ringling Brothers circus company was particularly known for using this phrase as a daily command to begin dismantling and moving its massive entertainment operation, which could include up to 100 railroad cars of equipment and performers.

Buckle down - To apply oneself with determination to a task
Origin: The phrase dates back to 16th-century sailing ships, first appearing in naval documents around 1570. It referred to the physical act of securing cargo or sails by "buckling down" the heavy leather straps that held them in place during storms. By the early 1700s, British naval officers had begun using it metaphorically to describe sailors focusing intently on their

duties. The phrase entered common usage through the influence of maritime language on everyday speech.

Push the envelope - To extend the boundaries of what is possible or conventional
Origin: This phrase originated in mathematics and aeronautical engineering in the 1940s. The "envelope" refers to the mathematical limits of aircraft performance—specifically, the graphed curve showing an aircraft's capabilities. Test pilots at Edwards Air Force Base in California popularized the phrase during the post-WWII era, with Chuck Yeager's breaking of the sound barrier in 1947 being perhaps the most famous example of literally "pushing the envelope."

As the crow flies - The shortest direct distance between two points
Origin: This phrase dates back to British coastal navigation in the early 18th century. Coastal vessels would carry crows aboard ships and release them when fogbound near land. The crow's instinct to fly straight toward the nearest shore helped guide ships to safety. The phrase first appeared in print in 1767 in A New Dictionary of the Terms Ancient and Modern of the Canting Crew. It was regularly used in maritime navigation logs before becoming common in general usage.

Riding shotgun - Sitting in the front passenger seat of a vehicle.
Origin: This phrase originates from the American Wild West in the 19th century when stagecoaches carried valuable cargo across dangerous territories. A guard, armed with a shotgun, would sit beside the driver to protect against bandits and outlaws. The term "riding shotgun" first appeared in print in

the early 1900s and became popularized through Western films and television, eventually evolving into a casual reference for sitting in the front seat of a car.

One for the road - A final drink before departing.
Origin: This phrase dates back to medieval England when condemned prisoners were sometimes given a final drink of ale before their execution. It became more commonly associated with drinking culture in the 20th century, especially in British pubs, where patrons would have a last round before heading home. The phrase gained widespread usage during the mid-1900s with the rise of automobile culture, cautioning against drinking before driving.

To run amuck - To behave uncontrollably or destructively.
Origin: This phrase comes from the Malay word "amok," which referred to a frenzied, violent outburst often attributed to warriors in Southeast Asia. The term was first introduced to English in the 16th century through European encounters with Malay culture. British colonial accounts from the 18th and 19th centuries further popularized the term, eventually leading to its modern figurative use for chaotic or reckless behavior.

To give something a wide berth - To avoid something or someone.
Origin: This phrase originates from nautical terminology dating back to the 17th century. "Berth" referred to the space a ship needed to maneuver safely while anchored or docked. Sailors would give dangerous coastlines, other vessels, or obstacles a "wide berth" to avoid collisions. The phrase gradually entered common usage to describe steering clear of trouble or undesirable situations.

On cloud nine - To be extremely happy or elated
Origin: The phrase is thought to have originated from the US Weather Bureau's cloud classification system in the 1950s, where "cloud nine" referred to cumulonimbus clouds reaching extraordinary heights. The term gained popularity in American culture in the late 1950s, appearing in songs and expressions. Though earlier idiomatic uses featured various numbers, "nine" became the standard, possibly influenced by associations with high-ranking states of joy or enlightenment in other contexts.

Wear your heart on your sleeve - To display one's emotions openly
Origin: This phrase originated from medieval jousting tournaments in the 1300s. Knights would wear a token (usually a handkerchief or ribbon) from their chosen lady on their sleeve during competition. The tradition began during the reign of Henry VIII, where knights would wear the color or emblem of the lady they were courting for an entire week

of festivities. Shakespeare later popularized the phrase in "Othello" (1604).

Have butterflies in your stomach - To feel nervous or anxious
Origin: This phrase likely emerged in the early 20th century as a description of the physical sensation of nervousness. The first documented uses appear in American newspapers from 1908 to 1912, often describing the feelings of performers before going on stage. The butterfly imagery might have been inspired by the fluttering sensation in the stomach caused by anxiety-induced digestion changes. By the 1950s, the phrase had become widespread in popular culture, particularly in describing pre-performance jitters or romantic nervousness.

Heart of gold - To have a kind, generous, and sincere nature
Origin: This metaphor dates back to medieval alchemy in the 12th century, when gold was considered the most perfect and precious metal. Chaucer used a similar phrase in The Canterbury Tales (1390s), but Shakespeare popularized the exact wording in Henry V (1599) with the line, "The king's a bawcock, and a heart of gold." Gold's association with moral purity and value made it a natural metaphor for goodness of character.

Fly off the handle - To become suddenly and extremely angry
Origin: This American phrase emerged in the early 1800s, referencing the dangerous phenomenon of loose axe heads flying off their wooden handles during use. The earliest printed reference appears in Thomas C. Haliburton's The Attaché (1843), which describes the hazards of poorly made axes in frontier settlements. The physical danger of a loose

axe head naturally evolved into a metaphor for losing one's temper.

Down in the dumps - To feel sad or depressed
Origin: This phrase originated in 15th century England, where "dump" referred to a state of confusion or haze, possibly related to Dutch "domp" (haze or mist). The first recorded use appears in a 1529 document by Thomas More, referring to being in "the dumps." The term gained popularity during the Tudor period, with "dumps" being used in several of Shakespeare's plays to describe melancholy states.

Blood boiling - Becoming extremely angry or enraged
Origin: This phrase originated from medieval humoral medicine theory, particularly prevalent in Europe during the 13th-15th centuries. According to Hippocratic and Galenic medical theories, an excess of blood (one of the four humors) would heat up and "boil" when a person became angry, causing their temperament to become choleric. The concept appeared in numerous medieval medical texts, including the influential 1235 work "De Proprietatibus Rerum" by Bartholomeus Anglicus. By the 17th century, the phrase had become commonly used in literature even as humoral theory fell out of medical practice.

Blow your top - To become extremely angry or lose one's temper
Origin: This phrase emerged in the early 1800s during the Industrial Revolution, inspired by the dangerous phenomenon of steam boiler explosions. Steam engines would literally "blow their tops" if pressure wasn't properly released, causing catastrophic accidents. The phrase first appeared in print in

American newspapers around 1820 and became widespread as steam power dominated industrial development.

Keep your cool - To remain calm and controlled in a difficult situation

Origin: This phrase emerged from African American jazz culture in the 1930s, where "cool" signified a specific style of relaxed performance and attitude. The phrase gained mainstream popularity during the 1950s Beat Generation movement. Jazz musicians first used it to describe maintaining composure during improvisational performances.

Put on a brave face - To maintain a cheerful appearance despite difficulties

Origin: This phrase emerged gradually in English during the 18th century, building on the long-standing use of "face" as a metaphor for outward appearance or demeanor. While theatrical traditions likely influenced its development, the first documented uses appear in personal letters and diaries from the 1750s to the 1760s. These letters and diaries describe social situations where people had to maintain composure despite personal difficulties. The phrase became common in Victorian literature, particularly in novels about social propriety and emotional restraint.

Seeing red - To become extremely angry or enraged

Origin: The phrase is commonly linked to Spanish bullfighting traditions, where matadors use red capes to provoke bulls. Although bulls are colorblind to red, the association of the color with anger became entrenched in popular culture. The idiom first appeared in English in the late 19th century and gained traction in the early 20th century, reflecting a broader symbolic link between red and heightened emotions.

Long face - A sad or disappointed expression
Origin: This phrase dates back to the 1700s when physiognomy (judging character from facial features) was popular in European society. The first documented use appears in a 1768 treatise on human expressions. The downward pull of facial muscles during sadness, creating an elongated appearance, led to this metaphorical description.

Thick-skinned - Not easily offended or affected by criticism
Origin: This phrase emerged from medieval hunting terminology in the 1400s, referring to animals with literally thick hides that were difficult to pierce. The first metaphorical use appears in a 1540 medical text comparing physical and emotional resilience. The phrase gained popularity during the Age of Enlightenment as scientific understanding of anatomy increased.

Have a chip on your shoulder - To maintain a grievance or feeling of resentment, often leading to a combative attitude
Origin: This phrase originated in 19th-century America, specifically around 1830. Young men would literally place a wood chip on their shoulder and dare others to knock it off, the act serving as a challenge to fight. The practice was first documented in the Long Island Telegraph on May 20, 1830, which described it as "being too ready to fight." The custom likely emerged from shipyards, where workers carried timber on their shoulders and challenged others who bumped into them.

Swallow your pride - To accept humiliation or embarrassment while remaining quiet about it

Origin: This metaphorical phrase dates back to the mid-1600s and draws parallels between one's pride and a bitter pill or unpleasant food that must be swallowed. The first documented use appears in Thomas Fuller's "The Church History of Britain" (1655), where he writes of "swallowing their private pride." The metaphor resonated strongly in an era when medicine was particularly unpalatable, and the act of swallowing something disagreeable was a common experience.

Heart of stone - To be cold, unfeeling, or lacking in compassion

Origin: This metaphor traces back to ancient religious texts, particularly the Old Testament book of Ezekiel (36:26), written around 600 BCE. The phrase contrasts a "heart of stone" with a "heart of flesh" in discussing spiritual transformation. It gained broader secular usage during the Middle Ages, appearing frequently in medieval romance literature where knights were described as having hearts "harder than stone" when resistant to love. The metaphor persisted through Shakespeare's works and became firmly established in common usage.

Burst into tears - To suddenly begin crying, usually due to intense emotion

Origin: The phrase emerged in the late 1500s, with one of the earliest recorded uses appearing in Edmund Spenser's "The Faerie Queene" (1590). The word "burst" in this context derives from the Old English "berstan," meaning to break suddenly. The metaphorical connection between intense emotions and bursting vessels or containers was particularly resonant in Renaissance literature, where the body was often viewed as a container for humor and passion.

Ticked off - To be angry, irritated, or annoyed
Origin: This American slang expression emerged in the early 1900s, possibly derived from "tick," a minor irritation like an insect. The first printed uses appeared in American newspapers in the 1910s, initially hyphenated as "ticked-off." Some etymologists connect it to checking items off a list, suggesting the idea of being "marked" or "noted" for punishment, though this connection remains speculative.

At your wit's end - To be utterly frustrated and unable to think of what to do next
Origin: This phrase appears in the 1611 King James Bible translation of Psalm 107:27, which describes sailors in a storm who "are at their wit's end." The term "wit" in this context refers to mental faculty or understanding, derived from the Old English "wit," meaning intelligence or mind. The metaphor of reaching the physical end of one's mental resources was particularly powerful in an era when maps literally showed the edge of the known world.

Keep your hair on - To stay calm and not lose one's temper
Origin: This British phrase emerged in the mid-1800s during the height of wig-wearing fashion among the upper classes. The first documented use appears in Pierce Egan's "Real Life in London" (1821). The phrase plays on the image of someone becoming so agitated that their wig might fall off, a genuinely embarrassing social faux pas in an era when maintaining a dignified appearance was paramount. By the 1850s, it had become a common colloquial expression even as wig-wearing

declined. It likely influenced the similar American term "keep your shirt on."

Keep your shirt on - To remain calm and patient; to not get angry or upset.
Origin: This phrase dates back to 19th-century America, where men would often remove their shirts before engaging in a physical fight, especially in heated arguments or brawls. Telling someone to "keep their shirt on" was a way of advising them to stay calm and avoid escalating the situation. Over time, it became a common idiom for urging patience and restraint in any context, not just physical altercations.

Resting on your laurels - Relying on past achievements instead of striving for further success.
Origin: This phrase originates from ancient Greece and Rome, where victorious athletes and military leaders were awarded laurel wreaths as symbols of honor. By the Middle Ages, "resting on one's laurels" had taken on a figurative meaning, suggesting complacency after success. The phrase was widely used in literature by the 19th century to criticize those who stopped making an effort after achieving recognition.

Rub the wrong way - To irritate or annoy someone.
Origin: This phrase is believed to originate from colonial America, where rubbing wooden floors against the grain would cause damage and create an unpleasant texture. Another theory ties it to petting a cat against the natural direction of its fur, which often annoys the animal. By the early 19th century, the phrase was commonly used in literature to describe interpersonal friction and annoyance.

Goody two shoes - A person who is excessively virtuous or well-behaved.
Origin: This phrase comes from the 1765 children's book *The History of Little Goody Two-Shoes*, attributed to John Newbery. The story follows an orphan girl who only has one shoe but is later given a full pair, symbolizing her improvement in life. Over time, the phrase shifted to describe someone who acts overly righteous or eager to please authority figures.

Hands down - Easily or without question.
Origin: This phrase comes from horse racing in the 19th century, where a jockey who was far ahead in a race could relax and lower their hands, no longer needing to urge the horse forward. The phrase was first recorded in sporting commentary in the mid-1800s and later broadened to describe any easy or unquestioned victory.

Go around your thumb to get to your finger - To take an unnecessarily complicated route to achieve something simple.
Origin: This lesser-known idiom likely originated as a metaphor in early American or British English, referencing the inefficiency of navigating one's own hand in a roundabout way. While its documented origins are unclear, the phrase follows a long tradition of proverbs highlighting indirect and unnecessary effort, similar to "taking the long way around."

Namby pamby - Weak, overly sentimental, or childish.
Origin: This phrase originated in the early 18th century as a satirical nickname for English poet Ambrose Philips, who was mocked for writing excessively delicate and sentimental verses. The term was coined by poet Henry Carey in 1725 and quickly became a popular expression for anything seen as

feeble or overly delicate. By the 19th century, "namby pamby" was widely used in literature and speech to ridicule weakness or excessive sentimentality.

LIFE & DEATH

Pushing up daisies - To be dead and buried
Origin: This phrase gained widespread use during World War I among British soldiers in the trenches. First recorded in soldiers' letters from 1917, it reflected the grim humor of troops facing mortality daily. The phrase references the fact that daisies commonly grow on cemetery grounds, particularly in Europe, and the flowers' roots would grow downward toward buried bodies.

Saved by the bell - Rescued from a difficult situation at the last possible moment
Origin: This phrase originated in boxing in the late 19th century. When a boxer was close to losing, the bell signaling the end of a round would "save" them from defeat. The first documented use appears in the sporting press of the 1930s. Contrary to popular belief, it has no connection to being buried alive with a bell system, which is a modern urban legend.

Kick the bucket - To die

Origin: This phrase dates to 18th-century England, first appearing in print in 1785 in Francis Grose's Dictionary of the Vulgar Tongue. The term likely derives from the method of livestock slaughter in which animals were hung from a wooden beam (called a bucket). In their death throes, the animals would kick the bucket with their legs. Some etymologists also connect it to the Old French word 'buquet,' meaning a balance or beam.

Cheat death - To narrowly escape or survive a potentially fatal situation

Origin: This phrase dates back to medieval European folklore and literature, particularly in stories where characters would outsmart or bargain with Death personified. The concept gained prominence in the 15th century with morality plays like Everyman (c. 1485), in which Death was portrayed as a character who could be temporarily outmaneuvered. The modern phrase became widely used after appearing in numerous literary works during the Renaissance period.

Over my dead body - Something that will not be allowed to happen under any circumstances

Origin: The phrase first appeared in print in the early 1800s, notably in Sir Walter Scott's novel The Antiquary (1816). It evolved from the ancient practice of defenders literally lying across thresholds or boundaries to prevent enemies from crossing. This dramatic form of protest was documented in medieval European chronicles and became a metaphor for absolute opposition.

Dead as a doornail - Completely and irrevocably dead
Origin: This phrase appears in William Langland's Piers Plowman (1362), making it one of the oldest recorded English idioms still in use. It refers to the practice of securing doors with nails that were "dead" or clinched, meaning they were hammered flat on the inside and couldn't be removed for reuse. Shakespeare later used it in Henry VI (1592), helping to cement its place in common usage.

On your last legs - Near the end of life or usefulness
Origin: This phrase dates to the late 16th century, first appearing in Thomas Nashe's "Have with You to Saffron-Walden" (1596). It originally referred to furniture legs wearing out but quickly evolved to describe both people and objects nearing their end. The phrase became widespread during the Industrial Revolution as machinery became more common.

Give up the ghost - To die or cease functioning
Origin: This phrase comes from biblical translations, specifically appearing in the King James Bible (1611) but dating back to Wycliffe's translation (1382). It derives from the ancient belief that the spirit or "ghost" leaves the body at death. The phrase began appearing in secular contexts during the 17th century and later extended to machines ceasing to function.

Last gasp - The final moment or effort before death or failure
Origin: This phrase emerged in medical literature of the 1630s, describing the death rattle or final breath of dying patients. First documented in Thomas Johnson's "Gerard's Herball" (1633), it gradually evolved from literal to

metaphorical usage. By the 1800s, it was commonly used to describe any final effort or moment before failure.

Cross over - To pass from one state to another, particularly from life to death
Origin: This phrase originated in ancient Egyptian mythology, where the dead were believed to cross the River Nile to reach the afterlife. The concept was later adopted by Greek mythology with the River Styx, where the ferryman Charon would transport souls across the water for a fee (hence the tradition of placing coins on the deceased's eyes). The phrase first appeared in English religious texts during the 14th century, referring to the soul's journey from life to death.

Bought the farm - To die, especially in military service
Origin: This phrase emerged among American airmen during World War II. The government's life insurance payout for a fallen soldier was typically enough to pay off a family farm's mortgage. First documented in military communications, it reflected the common dream among servicemen of eventually settling down on a farm after their service.

Drop dead gorgeous - Extremely attractive
Origin: This American slang phrase emerged in the 1960s, first appearing in fashion magazines describing stunning models. It combines the 1920s slang "drop dead" (meaning to be astonished) with "gorgeous." The phrase reflected the dramatic language of fashion and entertainment media during the period and became mainstream by the 1970s.

Death warmed over - Looking extremely ill, tired, or unwell
Origin: This vivid expression emerged in American English during the 1850s influenza epidemics. It was first documented in New England medical journals, where doctors described

patients as looking like "death warmed over" to indicate a severe state between life and death. The phrase gained widespread use during the devastating 1857-1858 influenza pandemic when Boston physician James Jackson used it in his published case studies. The metaphor compares someone's sickly appearance to a corpse that has been temporarily reanimated or "warmed," reflecting the period's growing scientific interest in the nature of death and reanimation.

Dead ringer - An exact duplicate or replica
Origin: This phrase originated in horse racing circles during the 1880s, stemming from the practice of substituting a faster horse for a slower look-alike to manipulate betting odds. The term "ringer" was already being used in American racing circles to describe a horse substituted for another in fraudulent betting schemes, while "dead" was used to mean "exact" or "precise" (as in "dead center"). The first documented use appeared in the Manitoba Daily Free Press in 1882, and the phrase became widespread in American sporting circles by the 1890s. There is a common misconception that the phrase comes from people being buried alive with bells, but this is historically unfounded.

Meeting your maker - To die, especially suddenly or unexpectedly
Origin: This euphemism emerged from Christian theological traditions in the Middle Ages, first appearing in religious texts from the 14th century. The phrase reflects the biblical concept of returning to God after death and became more commonly used in secular contexts during the Protestant Reformation of the 16th century when religious language entered everyday speech.

Life of Riley - A luxurious or carefree existence

Origin: This phrase originated from a popular American radio show called "The Life of Riley" that first aired in 1941, starring William Bendix as Chester A. Riley, a wing riveter living a comfortable blue-collar life. However, the expression itself predates the show, appearing in Irish-American vernacular as early as 1911. The term may have its roots in the real-life story of Pat Rooney, an Irish-American vaudeville performer who gained fame in the 1880s for a song celebrating the prosperous life of a man named Riley. The phrase gained widespread popularity during the post-World War II economic boom when the American middle class began enjoying unprecedented prosperity.

Last straw - The final problem or difficulty that makes a situation unbearable

Origin: This is a shortened version of "The Last Straw that Broken the Camel's Back," first recorded in Charles Dickens's Dombey and Son (1848). The concept draws from the ancient Arabic proverb about carefully loading camels with straw until a single additional piece causes collapse. The metaphor appeared in various forms in Turkish and Persian texts dating back to the 13th century before being popularized in English through trade routes.

Six feet under - Dead and buried

Origin: This phrase stems from London's 1665 plague outbreak when Mayor Sir John Lawrence ordered all graves to be dug at least six feet deep to help prevent the spread of disease. The decree was part of the "Orders Conceived and Published by the Lord Mayor and Aldermen of the City of London Concerning the Infection of the Plague." This depth became standard practice throughout England and its colonies, eventually spreading to much of the Western world.

A fate worse than death - A terrible situation or outcome considered to be even more undesirable than dying
Origin: This dramatic phrase emerged in Gothic literature of the late 18th century, particularly in works dealing with perceived threats to female virtue. Ann Radcliffe's 1794 novel The Mysteries of Udolpho helped popularize the phrase, which referred to the potential dishonor facing the heroine. The term gained widespread use during the Victorian era, appearing frequently in melodramas and sensation novels of the 1800s.

Rest in peace - A phrase expressing the hope that someone's soul finds eternal peace after death
Origin: Derived from the Latin "requiescat in pace," this phrase first appeared in 8th-century Christian catacombs in Rome. It was originally written as "R.I.P." on Catholic gravestones, representing a prayer for the soul's peaceful repose until the Day of Judgment. The practice spread throughout Europe during the Medieval period, becoming standard on Christian tombstones by the 1700s.

As dead as a dodo - Completely extinct or obsolete.
Origin: This phrase originates from the dodo, a flightless bird native to Mauritius that became extinct by the late 1600s due to hunting and introduced predators. The expression "as dead as a dodo" emerged in the 19th century as a metaphor for anything that had completely vanished or become irrelevant. The phrase gained popularity in British literature, reinforcing the dodo as a symbol of irreversible extinction.

As dead as a doorknob - Completely and unquestionably dead.

Origin: This phrase dates back to at least the 16th century, with early versions appearing in English literature, including Shakespeare's *Henry VI, Part 2* (1592). "Doorknob" (sometimes "doornail") was used metaphorically to emphasize absolute lifelessness, as nails and knobs were inanimate objects. The phrase became widely used in the 18th and 19th centuries to describe complete finality.

A shot in the arm - Something that boosts morale, energy, or success.

Origin: This phrase dates back to the early 20th century and originates from medical injections that provided quick relief or stimulation, such as morphine or vaccines. By the 1920s, "a shot in the arm" was being used metaphorically in American newspapers to describe anything that provided an immediate boost, such as financial investments or motivational actions. The phrase remains a common expression for a revitalizing or encouraging influence.

TIME & CHANGE

In the nick of time - At the last possible moment, just before it's too late

Origin: This phrase, dating back to the 1580s, refers to nick marks on tally sticks used for precise time measurements. These marks were notches cut into wood or metal to measure time in small increments. Shakespeare used the phrase in "The Merry Wives of Windsor" (1600), helping popularize it. By the late 17th century, the term had evolved from literal time measurement to metaphorical usage.

Time flies - Time passes quickly, especially when engaged in something pleasant

Origin: This is a translation of the Latin phrase "tempus fugit," which first appeared in Virgil's Georgics, Book III, line 284, around 29 BCE. The full Latin phrase was "tempus fugit irreparabile" meaning "irretrievable time flies." The phrase entered common English usage during the Renaissance period when Latin scholarly works were being translated and incorporated into English literature.

Against the clock - Racing to meet a deadline; hurrying to finish something on time

Origin: This phrase emerged in the late 19th century with the standardization of time measurement and the rise of industrial efficiency. The first documented uses appeared in sporting contexts around 1880, particularly in cycling and running events where competitors raced to beat specific times rather than each other. The phrase became more common with the advent of modern workplace time management.

Better late than never - It's preferable to do something after the expected time than not at all

Origin: This proverb traces back to Geoffrey Chaucer's "Canterbury Tales" written in the late 14th century, specifically appearing in "The Yeoman's Tale." The Latin version "potius sero quam nunquam" dates even earlier. Chaucer's use helped establish it as a common English phrase during the Middle Ages.

Race against time - To compete with time to accomplish something before a deadline

Origin: This phrase gained prominence during the Industrial Revolution of the 19th century when factory efficiency and time management became crucial. The first documented uses appear in newspaper accounts of rescue efforts and medical emergencies in the 1850s. The phrase reflected the increasing importance of time measurement in Victorian society and the growing pressure to accomplish tasks within strict deadlines.

Once in a blue moon - Very rarely; infrequently

Origin: This phrase dates back to the 16th century when the term "blue moon" referred to an extra full moon in a season. The Maine Farmers' Almanac (1937) defined it as the third full moon in a season with four full moons rather than the usual three. The phrase gained widespread use in the 19th century as a way to describe rare events.

Like clockwork - Operating with perfect regularity and precision

Origin: This simile emerged in the late 18th century when mechanical clocks became more precise and reliable. The phrase gained popularity during the Industrial Revolution, particularly after the development of chronometers by John Harrison in the 1760s. It reflected the era's growing fascination with mechanical precision and reliability.

Time is money - Time is a valuable resource that should not be wasted

Origin: Benjamin Franklin first coined this phrase in his 1748 essay "Advice to a Young Tradesman." The exact quote was, "Remember that time is money. He that can earn ten shillings a day by his labor, and goes abroad, or sits idle one half of that day... has really spent five shillings." The phrase reflected the emerging capitalist mindset of Colonial America and the Protestant work ethic.

On borrowed time - Living or continuing beyond the expected time of death or end

Origin: This phrase emerged in the late 19th century, first appearing in American literature of the 1870s. It likely originated from the practice of borrowing time payments, where missing a payment meant forfeiture. The phrase gained prominence during World War I as soldiers used it to describe their survival in dangerous conditions.

Crack of dawn - The very beginning of daylight, very early morning

Origin: This phrase first appeared in American English in the early 19th century. It likely originated from the visual metaphor of daylight "cracking" through the darkness like a crack in a wall. The phrase was commonly used in rural and farming contexts by the 1820s, reflecting agricultural society's early rising habits.

Eleventh hour - The latest possible moment before a deadline
Origin: This phrase originates from the biblical Parable of the Workers in the Vineyard (Matthew 20:1-16), written in the 1st century CE. In the parable, workers hired at the eleventh hour (5 PM) received the same wages as those who worked all day. The term became especially common during the Industrial Revolution when factory shifts were strictly timed. The first secular printed use appears in the early 1800s.

Time waits for no one - Time passes regardless of what anyone does or wants
Origin: This is a modernization of the medieval phrase "time and tide wait for no man." The shorter version emerged in the 16th century and appears in John Lyly's "Euphues" (1578). The phrase reflects the Renaissance period's growing awareness of time as a finite resource and the increasing importance of punctuality in urban society.

Beat the clock - To finish or accomplish something before a deadline
Origin: This phrase emerged in the 1940s with the rise of radio and television game shows. The term gained widespread popularity through the CBS game show "Beat the Clock," which debuted in 1950 and was hosted by Bud Collyer. Contestants would perform tasks within a strict time limit,

making the concept literal before it evolved into a general metaphor for racing against deadlines.

Dawn of time - Referring to the very beginning of existence or history.
Origin: The phrase "dawn of time" has its roots in ancient literature, with early associations found in religious texts and creation myths. It gained prominence in the 18th century during the Romantic period, as poets and philosophers used the imagery of dawn to symbolize beginnings and enlightenment. The word "dawn" itself, indicating the first light of day, is derived from the Old English "dagian." By the 19th century, it was firmly established in literature and discourse to evoke the origins of the world or human history.

Out of time - Having no time left or being late.
Origin: The concept of being "out of time" dates back to medieval England, where time was increasingly regulated by clocks in public spaces. The phrase gained traction in the 16th and 17th centuries with the rise of theatrical works, especially in Shakespearean plays where characters often lament their lack of time for crucial tasks. By the Industrial Revolution, "out of time" became a common expression, reflecting the growing emphasis on punctuality and schedules.

Two shakes of a lamb's tail - Very quickly or in a short amount of time.
Origin: This whimsical idiom emerged in rural England during the 18th century, inspired by the natural quick movements of lambs. Farmers noticed the characteristic way lambs flicked their tails in rapid, jerky motions. Author Jonathan Swift first documented the phrase in a letter, using it

humorously to convey brevity. Over time, it evolved into a playful way to describe promptness or speed.

Against the time - Preparing for a specific moment or deadline.

Origin: This expression has biblical origins, appearing in translations of scripture as early as the 16th century. It was used to emphasize readiness for a foreordained event, often with religious or moral implications. By the 19th century, it had entered secular usage, particularly in legal and military contexts, to indicate preparation against a future eventuality.

Time immemorial - A time so long ago that it is beyond memory or record.

Origin: The term originates from English common law, where it was used to denote a point in time beyond legal memory, specifically before the reign of King Richard I in 1189. The phrase "time immemorial" began appearing in legal texts during the 13th century and later entered literary and colloquial usage. It reflects the medieval mindset of defining history with fixed starting points while also capturing a poetic sense of ancient and forgotten eras.

Make time - To find or set aside time for something despite being busy.

Origin: The phrase "make time" was first recorded in the 16th century, coinciding with the Renaissance's focus on productivity and personal agency. Writers like William Shakespeare used the phrase to convey the deliberate allocation of time for important matters. Its enduring usage reflects changing attitudes toward time management, particularly as industrialization placed greater emphasis on scheduling and efficiency.

Kill time - To engage in activities that pass the time while waiting for something.

Origin: "Kill time" emerged in the 18th century during the Enlightenment, as leisurely pastimes became more common among the upper classes. The phrase metaphorically likens time to an adversary that needs to be subdued. Early literary uses, such as in the works of Samuel Johnson, highlight its application in describing idleness or unproductive waiting. The idiom gained popularity with the advent of modern transportation and urban life, where delays and downtime became more frequent.

The whole shebang - The entire thing; everything involved.

Origin: The exact origin of this phrase is debated, but "shebang" first appeared in American English in the mid-19th century. It was used by soldiers during the Civil War to refer to temporary shelters or structures. Mark Twain popularized the phrase in *Roughing It* (1872), and by the late 19th century, "the whole shebang" came to mean an entire affair or situation.

The whole nine yards - To give everything or make a full effort.

Origin: The precise origin of this phrase remains uncertain, but it gained popularity in American English during the 20th century. One theory links it to WWII fighter pilots, who allegedly had nine yards of ammunition belts and would fire them completely in battle. Another theory connects it to textile measurements or Scottish kilts. Though its exact roots remain unclear, the phrase was widely used in print by the 1960s to mean going all out.

Not for all the tea in China - Not for any amount of money or persuasion.

Origin: This phrase emerged in early 20th-century British English, reflecting China's dominance in global tea production. By the late 19th century, China supplied the majority of the world's tea, making it a symbol of immense wealth. The idiom suggests that no amount of riches—symbolized by China's vast tea resources—could persuade someone to take a particular action. It gained popularity in English-speaking countries by the mid-20th century.

Run of the mill - Ordinary, average, or unremarkable.

Origin: This phrase originates from the textile industry in the late 19th century. "Run of the mill" referred to goods produced directly from the mill without special selection or refinement. By the early 20th century, the phrase expanded beyond manufacturing to describe anything standard, unexceptional, or lacking unique qualities.

Throw in the towel - To give up or surrender
Origin: This phrase emerged from boxing in the 1910s. Historically, a boxer's seconds (assistants) would throw a towel into the ring to signal that their fighter could no longer continue, protecting them from further harm. The practice evolved from the earlier use of throwing up a sponge, which was documented in Pierce Egan's "Boxiana" (1812). The metaphorical use became common in the 1940s.

Keep your nose to the grindstone - To work hard and continuously at something
Origin: This phrase originated from medieval grain mills, where millers would check the quality of grinding by putting their noses close to the millstone to smell if the grain was being ground correctly. The earliest recorded use appears in a letter from 1532 in the British State Papers. By the 1700s, it had become a common metaphor for dedicated work.

Strike while the iron is hot - Take advantage of an opportunity immediately while conditions are favorable
Origin: This expression comes from blacksmithing practices dating back to ancient times. Medieval blacksmiths had to shape iron when it reached a specific temperature, typically between 2200-2350°F, making it malleable enough to work. The phrase first appeared in Geoffrey Chaucer's "Canterbury Tales" (circa 1386) and became widespread in the 14th century as blacksmithing was central to medieval European society.

Back to the drawing board - To start over after a failed attempt
Origin: This phrase originated from a 1941 New Yorker cartoon by Peter Arno. The cartoon shows a crashed plane and an engineer walking away, saying, "Well, back to the old drawing board." The phrase gained wider usage during the rapid technological development of World War II, when military projects often required multiple design iterations. It reflected the iterative nature of engineering and design work during wartime innovation.

Learn the ropes - To learn the basics of a job or activity
Origin: This nautical phrase originated in the age of sail (1700s), when new sailors had to learn the complex system of ropes controlling a ship's sails. The first documented metaphorical use appears in Richard Dana's "Two Years Before the Mast" (1840). As sailing declined in the late 1800s, the phrase transitioned to general use while maintaining its meaning of mastering basics.

Pull your weight - To contribute one's fair share of effort
Origin: This nautical phrase originated in the early 1800s on sailing ships. Crew members were expected to literally pull their own weight when hauling ropes and raising sails. The phrase first appeared in print in sailing manuals from the 1830s and, by the 1850s, had evolved into general use as a metaphor for doing one's fair share of work.

Cut corners - To do something in the easiest or cheapest way
Origin: This phrase originated from horse-drawn carriage driving in the 1800s, when drivers would literally cut corners too closely to save time. The first metaphorical use appears in transportation company records from the 1870s. The phrase gained wider usage during the efficiency movement of the early 1900s.

Cut from the same cloth - To be very similar in character or nature
Origin: This expression originated in the textile industry of 17th century England. When tailors made matching garments, they would cut pieces from the same bolt of fabric to ensure identical color and pattern, as dye lots could vary significantly. The phrase first appeared in written records around 1630 and became common in merchant correspondence about fabric quality and matching garments for wealthy patrons.

Climb the corporate ladder - To advance in rank or status within an organization
Origin: This phrase emerged during the rapid industrialization of the 1870s-1880s, when corporations began developing more structured hierarchies. The metaphorical "ladder" concept was first documented in business journals in the 1920s, coinciding with the rise of scientific management

principles developed by Frederick Taylor. The term became widespread during the post-WWII economic boom when corporate careers became increasingly standardized.

Call it a day - To stop working on something and continue at a later time
Origin: This phrase originated in the early 1800s as "call it half a day," appearing first in Lancaster Records of 1838 in Pennsylvania. The expression emerged during the Industrial Revolution when factory workers would negotiate for shorter working hours, with early departures being called "half days." By the 1870s, the shortened version of "call it a day" became common in British and American industrial working environments, reflecting the growing labor movement's influence on workplace culture.

Rise through the ranks - To advance in position or status by working one's way up from the bottom
Origin: This military phrase dates back to the 16th-century British Army system, where soldiers would literally advance from private to higher positions. The term "ranks" originally referred to the rows of foot soldiers arranged by their level of experience and skill. The first documented use appears in military documents from 1815 during the Napoleonic Wars, specifically in Wellington's dispatches. The phrase gained broader civilian usage during the Victorian era as businesses adopted military-style organizational structures.

All hands on deck - A call for everyone to help or participate in an effort
Origin: This nautical command originated in the British Royal Navy during the mid-1700s. Ship captains would use this call when all crew members, regardless of their regular

duties, were needed on the main deck for emergencies or battles. The phrase appears in Captain John Smith's "A Sea Grammar" (1627), though in a slightly different form. The exact modern phrasing first appeared in ship logs from the 1740s during the War of Jenkins' Ear, when British naval vessels frequently needed full crew participation.

Get down to business - To begin focusing on serious or important matters
Origin: This idiom emerged from merchant terminology in the late 1800s, specifically from the practice of physically sitting down to review accounting books and ledgers. The first printed usage appears in The Manchester Guardian in 1838, describing merchant meetings. The phrase gained popularity during the rapid commercial expansion of the Victorian era when formal business meetings became increasingly common in both Britain and America. The metaphorical meaning of focusing on serious matters evolved from this literal practice of merchants sitting down to examine their accounts.

Pink slip - A notice of dismissal from employment.
Origin: The term "pink slip" dates back to the early 1900s in the United States, particularly in industrial and clerical workplaces. It is believed that dismissal notices were printed on pink paper to distinguish them from other documents, making it easy for workers to identify the unwelcome news. While there is no definitive evidence of pink slips being universally used, the phrase gained popularity through cultural references and became a widely recognized term for termination.

Glass ceiling - An invisible barrier preventing women and minorities from advancing to higher positions in an organization.

Origin: The term "glass ceiling" first appeared in the late 20th century, specifically in a 1986 Wall Street Journal article addressing workplace inequality. It metaphorically describes the transparent but seemingly unbreakable barrier that limits career advancement for certain groups. The phrase gained traction during discussions of gender and racial equity in the corporate world, symbolizing systemic discrimination despite outward claims of equality.

Golden handcuffs - Financial incentives designed to keep employees tied to a company.

Origin: This phrase emerged in the 1970s during a period of corporate expansion and competitive talent retention strategies. Companies offered lucrative bonuses, stock options, and other benefits to discourage employees from leaving. The imagery of "golden handcuffs" highlights the allure and constraint of these incentives, as they often made leaving financially impractical despite potential job dissatisfaction.

Tool of the trade - A skill, piece of equipment, or resource essential to one's profession.

Origin: This idiom dates back to medieval times when craftsmen were required to own specific tools to practice their trade. Guilds, which regulated trades, often inspected the tools to ensure quality and compliance with standards. The phrase "tools of the trade" evolved to encompass not only physical instruments but also skills or knowledge indispensable to a profession.

Under the hammer - To be sold at an auction.
Origin: This expression originates from the auction process, where auctioneers use a hammer to signal the final bid. The practice of using a hammer dates back to 17th-century England, with documented instances in the early 1700s. The phrase "under the hammer" became synonymous with items being sold, emphasizing the decisive act of the hammer strike in confirming the sale.

Polish off - To finish something quickly or completely.
Origin: This phrase originated in the early 19th century, with "polish" used metaphorically to mean "to perfect or complete." Its usage expanded in casual language to denote efficiently finishing food, tasks, or other activities. The term carries a sense of thoroughness derived from the literal act of polishing to achieve a gleaming finish.

Carve out a niche - To establish a unique position or specialization in a particular field.
Origin: This idiom draws from the literal act of carving, which dates back to ancient times when artisans created specific spaces or designs in wood, stone, or other materials. The metaphorical usage began appearing in the 19th century, reflecting the growing emphasis on individuality and specialization during the industrial and professional expansion. "Carve out a niche" signifies the effort and precision required to secure a distinct and lasting place in a competitive environment.

Have your work cut out for you - To face a difficult or demanding task.
Origin: This phrase dates back to the 18th century and originates from tailoring, where fabric was "cut out" before

being sewn into garments. If a tailor had their work cut out, it meant they had a lot of material prepared and a significant amount of sewing ahead. By the 19th century, the phrase evolved into a metaphor for having a challenging or labor-intensive task to complete.

A feather in one's cap - A notable achievement or honor.
Origin: This phrase has roots in many cultures, where adding feathers to one's headdress signified bravery or accomplishment. In 16th-century Europe, victorious soldiers were often awarded feathers for their caps as a mark of distinction. Similar traditions existed among Indigenous American tribes and Mongolian warriors. The phrase became widely used in English literature by the 18th century as a metaphor for personal success or recognition.

A bigwig - An important or influential person.
Origin: This term originated in 17th- and 18th-century Europe when aristocrats and high-ranking officials wore large, elaborate wigs as a symbol of status. The bigger and more ornate the wig, the higher the rank of the wearer. By the 18th century, "bigwig" became a colloquial term for someone of great importance, and it remains a humorous way to describe powerful individuals today.

MONEY & COMMERCE

CASH COW

Cash cow - A business, investment, or product that provides a steady income or profits
Origin: The term emerged in the 1970s from the Boston Consulting Group's growth-share matrix, a business analysis tool. It was inspired by dairy cows that consistently produced milk with minimal maintenance costs. By the 1980s, the phrase quickly moved beyond business circles into general usage, appearing frequently in financial publications and mainstream media.

Break the bank - To exhaust one's financial resources or spend more than one can afford
Origin: This phrase originated in the gambling houses of Monte Carlo in the 1860s. When a gambler won more money than the house had available in its cash reserves, they were said to have "broken the bank." The casino would then cover the table with a black cloth until more money could be brought from their vault. The phrase gained wider use after

Fred Gilbert's 1892 song "The Man Who Broke the Bank at Monte Carlo" became a popular hit.

Money talks - Wealth and money have influence and power over situations and people

Origin: This phrase dates back to ancient Rome, where wealthy citizens could influence political decisions through financial contributions. The exact Latin phrase "pecunia loquitur" (money speaks) appeared in various Roman texts. The modern English version first appeared in print in the American Mercury magazine in 1926, though the concept was well-established in vernacular speech long before then.

Buck - A dollar; a unit of American currency.

Origin: The term originated during the American frontier period of the 1750s when deerskins ("buckskins") were commonly used as a currency for trading with Native Americans. A "buck" was standardized as the value of one male deerskin, which averaged around one dollar in trading posts. The earliest documented use appears in Conrad Weiser's 1750 journal about Native-American trade relations. The term gained widespread use during the California Gold Rush of the 1850s, when paper dollars became more common but retained the "buck" nickname from the earlier frontier era.

Cost an arm and a leg - To be extremely expensive

Origin: This colorful American phrase first appeared in the late 1940s during post-war inflation. While popular stories link it to portrait painters charging extra for painting limbs, the expression more likely emerged from the age-old idea of paying with body parts (similar to older phrases like "costing an eye"). The phrase caught fire in the 1950s as Americans grappled with rising consumer prices, perfectly capturing the feeling that some purchases required painful personal sacrifice.

Hit the jackpot - To achieve unexpected success or good fortune

Origin: The term originated in the 1880s from poker, where players would contribute to a pot that could only be won with a pair of jacks or better. The first documented use appeared in the Nevada State Journal in 1885. When slot machines were invented in the 1890s by Charles Fey, the term was adopted for the highest payout, which required lining up three bell symbols. The phrase entered common usage during the 1920s with the rise of mechanical gambling devices.

Money doesn't grow on trees - Money must be earned and isn't infinite or easily obtained

Origin: This saying emerged during the American Civil War era when the Confederate government printed excessive amounts of paper money, leading to severe inflation. The phrase was first recorded in an 1859 Missouri newspaper article warning about fiscal responsibility. It gained wider use during the Reconstruction era as a reminder of the value of hard work and financial prudence.

Pass the buck - To shift responsibility to someone else

Origin: This phrase originated from poker games in frontier America during the 1800s. A buckhorn-handled knife indicated the dealer's position, and players would "pass the buck" to the next dealer. The term gained political significance when President Truman placed a sign reading "The Buck Stops Here" on his desk in 1945.

Born with a silver spoon - Born into wealth and privilege
Origin: This phrase dates back to the Middle Ages when wealthy godparents gave silver spoons to their godchildren at christening ceremonies. The first documented use in English appears in a 1719 translation of Don Quixote. Silver spoons were valuable family heirlooms and symbols of inherited wealth, making them perfect metaphors for privilege.

Nest egg - Money saved for future use or emergency
Origin: This term comes from 18th-century chicken farmers who would place porcelain eggs in hens' nests to encourage laying. The practice was first documented in Thomas Tusser's "Five Hundred Points of Good Husbandry" (1573). The financial meaning emerged in the early 1800s, first appearing in American agricultural journals as a metaphor for saving money.

A King's Ransom - An enormous sum of money
Origin: This phrase originated from medieval European practices of ransoming captured royalty. The most famous example was the ransom of Richard I of England in 1192 when he was captured returning from the Third Crusade. The Holy Roman Emperor demanded 150,000 marks (about £2 billion in modern value), setting a historic precedent for the phrase's meaning of an excessive sum.

Double-edged sword - Something that has both positive and negative consequences
Origin: This metaphor dates back to the Roman Empire, where double-edged swords (gladius hispaniensis) were standard military equipment. The Latin phrase "anceps gladius" appears in Seneca's writings around 50 CE. The metaphorical meaning emerged during the Medieval period,

appearing in religious texts warning about the dual nature of power and wealth.

Foot the bill - To pay for something, often reluctantly or for others

Origin: This expression originated in the 18th-century British shipping industry. Ship's manifests would list expenses at the foot (bottom) of the page, and someone had to "foot" (add up and pay) these bills. The earliest printed use appears in the London Gazette of 1819, describing maritime accounting practices.

Money laundering - The act of concealing the origins of money obtained through illegal means by passing it through a complex sequence of banking transfers or commercial transactions.

Origin: The term became widely used in the 20th century, especially during the 1920s and 1930s, with organized crime syndicates like Al Capone's operation in Chicago. Its modern sense comes from the practice of using legitimate businesses, such as laundromats, to disguise illicit income. The first documented use of the term "money laundering" in its current meaning appeared in U.S. legal proceedings in the 1970s, particularly during the Watergate scandal. The phrase's evolution mirrors the increasing sophistication of financial crimes over time.

In the black - Operating at a profit or without financial debt.
Origin: This idiom comes from bookkeeping practices, where entries written in black ink signify positive financial figures, as opposed to red ink, which indicates losses. The practice dates back to at least the 19th century when ledgers were manually kept. The association with profitability became

common parlance in the early 20th century, particularly in reference to businesses showing annual gains. The idiom remains widely used in financial and everyday contexts.

Bits and Bobs - Small, miscellaneous items or tasks.
Origin: This British idiom is thought to have originated in the 18th century. It refers to scraps or fragments left over from larger items. "Bits" meant small pieces, while "bobs" was slang for odds and ends or small objects of low value. The phrase gained popularity during the 19th century, appearing in domestic and informal contexts. Its continued use reflects a longstanding cultural tendency to categorize unimportant or leftover things collectively.

Baker's dozen - A group of thirteen items, typically baked goods.
Origin: This phrase dates back to medieval England when bakers added an extra loaf or item to a dozen as insurance against penalties for shortchanging customers. In 1266, the Assize of Bread and Ale law regulated the price and weight of bread, imposing severe punishments for underweight loaves. To avoid these penalties, bakers would give thirteen instead of twelve, ensuring compliance. The term has since become a cultural relic of that historical practice.

Strike gold - To achieve sudden or unexpected success, often in a lucrative way.
Origin: The idiom originated during the California Gold Rush of 1848–1855 when prospectors would literally strike gold while mining, leading to instant wealth. The phrase was quickly adopted as a metaphor for achieving success in any endeavor. Early literary uses in American newspapers and writings from the mid-19th century helped popularize the

expression. Its enduring appeal lies in its association with fortune, ambition, and opportunity.

Penny-pincher - A person who is extremely reluctant to spend money, often to an unreasonable degree
Origin: This term originated in the mid-19th century during the era of widespread coin clipping, a form of currency debasement. In the 1850s, particularly in Britain and America, some people would actually "pinch" or shave off tiny amounts of metal from penny coins, collecting these shavings to sell as raw copper – a practice that was considered a form of theft. The first documented use appeared in an 1848 edition of the Boston Herald, where it was used literally to describe this illegal practice. By the 1860s, the term had evolved into a metaphor for general miserliness, as the idea of extracting value from the smallest unit of currency became symbolic of extreme frugality.

White elephant - A possession that is costly to maintain but has little practical value.
Origin: The phrase originates from the ancient kingdoms of Southeast Asia, particularly in Thailand and Burma, where rare white elephants were considered sacred. These elephants could not be put to work and required expensive upkeep. It is said that a king might gift a white elephant to a courtier as both an honor and a financial burden, leading to the modern meaning of the phrase. The term appeared in English literature by the mid-19th century to describe extravagant but impractical gifts or projects.

Ace in the hole - A hidden advantage or a secret resource.
Origin: This phrase comes from the game of poker, specifically stud poker, where players are dealt a concealed

"hole" card. If a player had an ace in the hole, they held a powerful, unseen advantage. The term became popular in American English in the late 19th and early 20th centuries, eventually expanding beyond poker to refer to any secret weapon or strategic advantage in various contexts.

A grain of salt - To view something with skepticism or caution.

Origin: The phrase traces its roots to ancient Rome, where the naturalist Pliny the Elder wrote about a remedy that included "a grain of salt" (*cum grano salis*) in *Naturalis Historia* (77 CE). The idea was that salt could help counteract poison, making it a symbol of cautious acceptance. The phrase entered English in the 17th century and evolved into its modern meaning of approaching claims or information with skepticism.

Crocodile tears - Insincere displays of sadness or remorse
Origin: This phrase originated from an ancient belief, first
recorded by Pliny the Elder in his "Natural History" (77 CE),
that crocodiles weep while eating their prey. Medieval
bestiaries widely circulated this belief, and it appeared in Sir
John Mandeville's 14th-century travel writings. Shakespeare
popularized the metaphorical meaning in Henry VI (1592),
cementing its use as a description of false grief.

Achilles' heel - A weakness or vulnerable point despite
overall strength
Origin: The phrase derives from Greek mythology,
specifically Homer's "Iliad" (circa 8th century BCE).
According to legend, when Achilles was born, his mother
Thetis dipped him in the River Styx to make him invulnerable
but held him by his heel, which remained vulnerable. This
story wasn't in Homer's original text but appeared in later
Roman sources, particularly Statius's "Achilleid" (circa 95

CE). The term became widely used in medical texts during the Renaissance period.

Open Pandora's box - To take an action that creates numerous unforeseen problems
Origin: This idiom comes from ancient Greek mythology, specifically Hesiod's "Works and Days" (circa 700 BCE). According to the myth, Zeus gave Pandora, the first woman on Earth, a box containing all the world's evils as a wedding gift, with instructions never to open it. Her curiosity led her to open the box, releasing all manner of evil and misfortune into the world, leaving only Hope at the bottom. The story served as a cautionary tale about divine punishment and human curiosity.

Midas touch - The ability to succeed in every financial or business venture
Origin: This phrase comes from the Greek myth of King Midas of Phrygia, first recorded by Ovid in Metamorphoses (8 CE). According to the tale, Dionysus granted Midas's wish that everything he touched would turn to gold. This initially seemed wonderful but became a curse when he couldn't eat or drink and accidentally transformed his daughter. Historical records confirm there was actually a King Midas who ruled Phrygia around 700 BCE, though his kingdom's great wealth likely inspired his legendary golden touch.

Knock on wood - To perform an action to avoid bad luck after mentioning good fortune
Origin: This superstition dates back to ancient Celtic and Germanic peoples who believed trees housed protective spirits. Touching or knocking on wood was a way to seek protection or thank the spirits for good fortune, with oak trees

being particularly sacred. The phrase first appeared in written English in the 1800s, though the practice is much older. British sailors often touched wooden ships' masts for luck, helping spread the custom globally.

Phoenix Rising - Something that emerges renewed from destruction
Origin: The phoenix myth originated in ancient Egyptian mythology with the Bennu bird, later adopted by the Greeks around 500 BCE. The earliest detailed account appears in Herodotus's "Histories" (440 BCE), describing a bird that regenerates cyclically every 500 years. Early Christians later adopted the symbol as a representation of resurrection and renewal.

Touch iron - To ward off bad luck (similar to knock on wood)
Origin: This superstition dates back to medieval Europe when people believed in the protective powers of iron against evil spirits and fairies. The practice was particularly strong in Celtic and Germanic regions, where iron was associated with strength and durability. Church doors often had iron fixtures that people would touch for protection, and the custom became especially common during the Black Death (1347-1351).

The third time's the charm - Success will come on the third attempt
Origin: This belief dates back to ancient British folklore and the rule of three in storytelling. The earliest written reference appears in Elizabeth Barrett Browning's letters from 1839. The phrase connects to medieval Christianity where three was considered a holy number due to the Trinity. It was also

influenced by the Latin phrase "omne trium perfectum" (everything that comes in threes is perfect).

Golden fleece - Something valuable and worth pursuing, often at great risk

Origin: This phrase comes from Greek mythology, specifically the story of Jason and the Argonauts, first recorded in Apollonius of Rhodes's "Argonautica" (3rd century BCE). The tale describes Jason's quest to retrieve a golden ram's fleece from Colchis. Historians suggest the myth may reflect historical gold-mining practices in the Black Sea region, where fleeces were used to trap gold particles from rivers.

Hair of the dog - Treating a hangover by drinking more alcohol

Origin: This phrase derives from an ancient belief, recorded in Pliny's "Natural History" (77 CE), that a bite from a rabid dog could be cured by applying hair from the same dog to the wound. The drinking connection first appeared in print in John Heywood's "A Dialogue Conteinyng Prouerbes" (1546). The practice became especially popular during the medieval period.

A Trojan horse - A person or thing intended to undermine or secretly overthrow from within

Origin: This phrase comes from Homer's epic poem "The Iliad," written around 800 BCE, describing the legendary Trojan War. After a decade-long siege of Troy, the Greeks constructed a massive wooden horse and left it outside the city gates while pretending to sail away. The Trojans brought the horse inside their walls as a victory trophy, unaware that Greek soldiers were hidden inside. Under cover of night, these soldiers emerged and opened the city gates for the returned Greek army, leading to Troy's fall. The term was first applied to computer malware in 1974 by Daniel Edwards of the U.S. Air Force.

Evil eye - A malevolent look that can cause injury or misfortune
Origin: This belief dates back to ancient Mesopotamian texts from around 3000 BCE. The concept appears in the Sumerian incantation: "The eye that brings woe." Archaeological evidence includes evil eye amulets from ancient Egypt and Greece. The belief spread throughout the Mediterranean and Middle East, with detailed descriptions appearing in the Talmud (completed around 500 CE).

Skeleton key - A key designed to open many different locks
Origin: The term emerged in the late 18th century, first appearing in locksmith manuals around 1780. The name derives from the key's stripped-down or bare design, reduced to its essential parts like a skeleton. Master keys became particularly important during the Industrial Revolution when standardized lock systems were needed for factories and large buildings.

Sisyphean task - An endless and futile task that must be repeatedly performed with no possibility of completion
Origin: The phrase derives from Greek mythology, specifically the tale of Sisyphus, a king of Ephyra (now Corinth) in the 13th century BCE. As punishment for his deceitfulness and hubris against the gods, Zeus condemned Sisyphus to eternally roll a boulder up a hill in the underworld, only to watch it roll back down each time he neared the top. The story was recorded in Homer's "Odyssey,"

and later philosophers, particularly Albert Camus, in his 1942 essay "The Myth of Sisyphus," used it as a metaphor for the human condition.

Speak with a forked tongue - To deliberately say one thing while meaning another; to lie or deceive
Origin: This phrase originated among Native American tribes, particularly the Navajo and Apache, in the 17th century. The metaphor compares a deceiver's tongue to a snake's forked tongue, which Native Americans observed could move in two different directions. The phrase gained widespread use during treaty negotiations between Native Americans and European settlers, with the first documented English usage appearing in James Fenimore Cooper's "The Last of the Mohicans" (1826).

Left in the lurch - To be abandoned or deserted in a difficult situation
Origin: The term originated from a 16th-century French dice game called "lourche," where a player who fell far behind was said to be "in the lourche." The word evolved into "lurch" in English and was later associated with cribbage and other games. By the 1590s, it had entered common usage in England to describe someone in a helpless position or disadvantageous situation. The first recorded non-gaming use appears in Thomas Nashe's "Have with You to Saffron-Walden" (1596).

Witch hunt - An intensive campaign to discover and persecute those with unpopular views or suspected wrongdoing
Origin: This phrase stems from the actual historical persecution of alleged witches, particularly during the European witch trials of the 15th through 17th centuries and

the Salem witch trials of 1692-93. The most intensive period was the "Great Witch Craze" (1450-1750), during which an estimated 40,000-60,000 people were executed. The term gained its modern metaphorical meaning during the McCarthy anti-communist investigations of the 1950s when Arthur Miller's play "The Crucible" (1953) used Salem as an allegory for McCarthyism.

Catch-22 - A paradoxical situation from which there is no escape due to contradictory circumstances
Origin: This term was coined by Joseph Heller in his 1961 novel Catch-22, set during World War II. In the book, crazy airmen were not obligated to fly dangerous missions, but requesting to be relieved of such duties was considered proof of sanity. The phrase was originally "Catch-18," but Heller's publisher requested the change to avoid confusion with Leon Uris's recently published "Mila 18." The term quickly entered common usage and was added to the Oxford English Dictionary in 1972.

Murphy's law - The adage that anything that can go wrong will go wrong
Origin: The phrase originated at Edwards Air Force Base in 1949 during Project MX981, which was designed to see how much sudden deceleration a person could stand in a crash. Captain Edward Murphy was a development engineer who discovered a technician had wired all 16 channels of a transducer incorrectly. Murphy reportedly remarked, "If there's more than one way to do a job, and one of those ways will result in disaster, somebody will do it that way." The project's safety officer, Major John Paul Stapp, popularized the term during a press conference.

Abracadabra - A magical phrase used to invoke supernatural powers or illusions.
Origin: The word "abracadabra" dates back to ancient Rome, first recorded in the 2nd century CE by the physician Serenus Sammonicus. He prescribed the term as an incantation to be written in a triangular pattern on amulets to ward off illness and evil spirits. The phrase's origins are debated, with some scholars suggesting it comes from Aramaic words meaning "I create as I speak." Over time, "abracadabra" became associated with stage magic and illusion, maintaining its mystical reputation.

As mad as a hatter - Completely crazy or eccentric.
Origin: This phrase originates from the 18th and 19th-century hat-making industry, particularly in England, where mercury was used to cure felt hats. Prolonged mercury exposure led to neurological damage, causing symptoms such as tremors, confusion, and erratic behavior, which became known as "mad hatter's disease." The phrase gained further popularity through Lewis Carroll's *Alice's Adventures in Wonderland* (1865), though it was already in use before the novel.

Blue blood - A person of noble or aristocratic lineage.
Origin: The term "blue blood" comes from the Spanish phrase *sangre azul*, which was used in medieval Spain to describe the nobility. The phrase emerged during the Reconquista (8th–15th century), as the ruling class, of primarily European descent, prided themselves on their fair skin, where veins appeared more visibly blue. The term spread to English by the 19th century, where it became a common way to refer to aristocracy and social elites.

Chasing rainbows - To pursue unrealistic goals
Origin: This phrase emerged from Celtic folklore and mythology in the 1800s. Irish legends told of leprechauns hiding gold at the end of rainbows. The first documented metaphorical use appears in an 1808 Irish folk collection. The phrase gained popularity during the California Gold Rush as a criticism of unrealistic get-rich-quick schemes.

Under the weather - Feeling ill or unwell
Origin: This nautical phrase originated in the 1800s as the shortened version of "under the weather bow," which refers to the side of a ship that takes the brunt of bad weather. Sailors who felt seasick would go below deck to protect themselves from the weather, leading to the phrase being associated with illness. The first printed use of the phrase appears in an 1850 edition of "The Congressional Globe."

Storm in a teacup - A great commotion over a minor problem
Origin: This phrase dates to the 1820s British tea culture, though similar expressions existed earlier in other languages.

The Dutch had "een storm in een glas water" (a storm in a glass of water) from the 1700s. The British version, reflecting their tea-drinking culture, first appeared in print in Catherine Sinclair's 1838 work "Modern Accomplishments." The American variation "tempest in a teapot" emerged in the 1850s.

Right as rain - Perfectly fine or correct
Origin: This alliterative phrase emerged in British Victorian society during the late 1800s, particularly in industrial cities like Manchester, where rain was remarkably reliable. The expression reflects a distinctly British perspective, where rain, though often unwelcome, represents dependability and natural order. Its widespread use in Victorian literature and everyday speech shows how agricultural metaphors persisted even as Britain became increasingly urban. The phrase first appeared in popular literature in the 1890s, quickly becoming a common expression for anything functioning perfectly or correctly.

Weather the storm - To survive a difficult period
Origin: This phrase originated from maritime vocabulary in the early 1600s. Ships would "weather" a storm by positioning themselves to minimize damage from wind and waves. The earliest documented use appears in Captain John Smith's "Sea Grammar" (1627). The phrase became common during the great age of sailing as stories of survival at sea captured the public imagination.

Fair-weather friend - Someone reliable only in good times
Origin: This phrase emerged from maritime culture in the mid-1700s. Sailors used "fair weather" to describe unreliable crew members who would only work in ideal conditions. The

first literary use of the phrase appears in Thomas Paine's The American Crisis (1776). The phrase gained widespread use during the American Revolution as a political criticism of those whose loyalty changed with circumstances.

Save for a rainy day - To set aside resources for future difficulties
Origin: This saying dates back to 16th-century England, when most workers were agricultural laborers paid only on days they could work. Rainy days meant no work and no pay, making savings essential. The earliest documented use appears in John Heywood's 1546 collection of proverbs. The phrase gained additional prominence during the agricultural depression of the 1730s.

Red sky at night - A weather prediction indicating fair weather the next day
Origin: This weather proverb dates back to ancient maritime cultures and appears in the Bible (Matthew 16:2-3). The first recorded English version appears in John Wodroephe's "The Spared Hours of a Soldier" (1623). The saying is based on actual atmospheric conditions: red skies at sunset often indicate high pressure and stable air approaching from the west in many parts of the world.

Snowed under - Overwhelmed with work or tasks
Origin: This phrase emerged during the American pioneer era of the 1880s. Early settlers in the Great Plains experienced severe winter storms that would literally bury their homesteads. The first metaphorical use appears in an 1880 edition of the "Nebraska State Journal." The phrase gained widespread use during the Industrial Revolution as office work became more common.

Head in the clouds - To be daydreaming or out of touch with reality

Origin: This idiom emerged during the Renaissance when clouds were associated with divine and philosophical contemplation. The earliest documented use appears in Christopher Marlowe's "Doctor Faustus" (1592), which describes scholarly distraction. The phrase became more common during the Romantic period of the late 1700s when poets often used cloud imagery to represent imagination and disconnection from worldly concerns.

Bolt from the blue - A sudden and unexpected event

Origin: This phrase dates to the early 1800s, referring to lightning strikes from clear blue skies, a rare but documented meteorological phenomenon called "heat lightning" or "dry lightning." The first notable appearance in literature was in Thomas Carlyle's 1837 work "The French Revolution," where he described sudden political upheavals as "bolts from the blue." The phrase gained popularity during the Victorian era as scientific understanding of atmospheric electricity improved, though sailors had long used similar expressions to describe unexpected storms.

Get wind of something - To hear or learn of something, especially secret information

Origin: This nautical expression originated in the 16th century among sailors and hunters who relied on wind direction to detect approaching vessels or prey. The phrase first appeared in nautical logs around 1540, as ship captains would note when they "got wind" of enemy vessels by observing the behavior of seabirds and wind patterns. By the 1700s, the phrase had evolved beyond maritime use to describe the acquisition of any kind of information, particularly through unofficial channels.

Take a rain check - To decline an offer now but accept it for a future time
Origin: This phrase emerged from American baseball in the 1880s. Baseball parks began issuing "rain checks" (substitute tickets) to spectators when games were postponed due to bad weather. The Philadelphia Athletics implemented the first documented rain check policy in 1885. By the early 1900s, the phrase had spread beyond baseball and entered common usage, particularly in retail, where stores would issue rain checks for out-of-stock items.

Storm brewing - An impending problem or trouble developing
Origin: The phrase originates from medieval English maritime traditions, first documented in ship logs from the 1650s. Sailors would observe specific cloud formations and air pressure changes to predict approaching storms, using the term "brewing" as an analogy to the familiar process of brewing ale, which also involved watching for specific signs of development. The metaphorical use appeared in Shakespeare's "The Tempest" (1610-1611), helping popularize it beyond nautical contexts.

Steal someone's thunder - To take credit for someone else's achievement or idea
Origin: This colorful phrase originated in early 18th-century British theater. In 1704, literary critic and playwright John Dennis invented a new method of creating thunder sound effects for his play "Appius and Virginia" at the Drury Lane Theatre. When the play failed, the theater reused his sound

effects in a production of "Macbeth" without his permission. Dennis famously complained, "Damn them! They will not let my play run, but they steal my thunder!" The incident was widely reported in London literary circles.

Rain on someone's parade - To spoil someone's plans or dampen their enthusiasm
Origin: This American phrase emerged from the tradition of civic and military parades in the late 19th century. The first documented use appears in local newspapers around 1898, describing actual rainstorms disrupting parades. The phrase gained popularity after World War I when many welcome-home parades for returning soldiers were affected by the weather. By the 1920s, it had evolved into a metaphor for any kind of spoiled celebration.

Break the ice - To initiate social interaction or overcome initial awkwardness
Origin: This phrase dates back to the age of northern European maritime trade in the 15th century. Special "ice-breaker" ships would be sent ahead of trading vessels to literally break up frozen waterways, allowing commerce to resume after winter. The first metaphorical use appears in Shakespeare's "The Taming of the Shrew" (1590), where breaking the ice represents overcoming social formality. The phrase became especially popular during the Victorian era's rigid social culture.

Throw caution to the wind - To act recklessly without concern for consequences
Origin: This phrase emerged from sailing terminology in the mid-17th century. Ships typically sailed with careful attention to wind patterns, but in desperate situations, they might

disregard these safety protocols. The earliest recorded use appears in Captain John Smith's 1629 sailing manual. The metaphorical meaning evolved during the Age of Exploration, as tales of daring sea voyages captured the public imagination.

Calm before the storm - A peaceful period before a time of trouble or upheaval
Origin: This phrase comes from ancient Mediterranean sailors' observations. Aristotle first documented the phenomenon in his "Meteorologica" (350 BCE), noting the unusual stillness that often precedes violent storms. The phrase entered English via translations of classical texts during the Renaissance. By the 16th century, it had become a common metaphor in political and social commentary, particularly in describing the lead-up to wars or revolutions.

Snow job - An elaborate deception or effort to convince through exaggeration or flattery
Origin: This phrase emerged from American military slang during World War II, first documented in print around 1943. The term likely arose from the metaphorical concept of obscuring the truth by blinding someone with a blizzard of words or false information, similar to how snow can reduce visibility. It gained widespread civilian use in the late 1940s, particularly in newspaper reporting and political commentary, reflecting the post-war period's growing concern with propaganda and public relations tactics.

To go haywire - To become uncontrollable, chaotic, or malfunctioning.
Origin: This phrase originated in the early 20th century and is linked to the use of haywire, a thin, easily tangled wire used for binding hay bales. Farmers and laborers often found that

haywire would twist and snarl unpredictably, leading to frustration. By the 1920s, the term was adopted in American slang to describe things going wrong or machinery malfunctioning, eventually expanding to describe chaotic situations in general.

Wet blanket - A person who dampens enthusiasm or fun. **Origin:** This phrase dates back to the early 19th century and originates from the literal use of wet blankets to smother fires. Firefighters and householders used them to extinguish flames, making the term a fitting metaphor for someone who stifles excitement. By the mid-1800s, the phrase was being used figuratively in English literature to describe individuals who discouraged others or dampened a lively atmosphere.

Basket case - Someone who is unable to function due to stress or nervous exhaustion.

Origin: This phrase originated during World War I and was first documented in U.S. military reports. It referred to soldiers who had lost all four limbs and were supposedly transported in baskets. Though there is no official confirmation that such cases existed, the phrase quickly evolved into a metaphor for someone emotionally or mentally overwhelmed. By the mid-20th century, "basket case" was widely used in both medical and colloquial contexts.

Pay through the nose - To pay an excessive amount
Origin: This phrase allegedly originated from the Danish conquest of Ireland in the 9th century, when they imposed a tax called "nose tax." While this origin is disputed, the first documented use appears in English tax records from the 1670s. The phrase became common during the South Sea Bubble financial crisis of 1720.

Wet behind the ears - Inexperienced; naive
Origin: This phrase comes from the observation that the last place to dry on a newborn animal is behind its ears. The first documented use appears in American farming journals from the 1850s. The phrase gained popularity during the late 1800s as urbanization made rural metaphors particularly appealing.

Rule of thumb - A rough practical principle or method
Origin: This phrase originated from medieval English carpentry, where craftsmen used their thumbs for approximate measurements. The first documented use appears in guild records from the 1500s. The phrase gained wider usage during the Industrial Revolution when precision measurements became more important. Ironically, it emphasizes the contrast with rough estimation.

Keep your head down - Stay out of trouble; avoid attracting attention
Origin: This phrase emerged from trench warfare during World War I (1914-1918). Military training manuals emphasized the importance of keeping one's head below the parapet to avoid sniper fire. British officer training documents from 1915 specifically stress this survival tactic. The metaphorical usage became common in civilian contexts during the 1920s.

Clean bill of health - A certification of good health or sound condition
Origin: This phrase originated in the Mediterranean maritime quarantine practices of the 1500s. Ships arriving at ports were required to present a "bill of health" signed by port authorities from their previous stops, confirming no plague or epidemics were present when they departed. A "clean" bill meant the port

of origin was disease-free, while a "foul" or "touched" bill indicated the presence of disease. The practice became standardized across European ports by the 17th century.

Gut feeling - An instinctive feeling or intuition
Origin: This phrase reflects ancient Greek medical theory from the 4th century BCE. Hippocrates and his followers believed the gut was the seat of emotions and intuition, a concept that persisted through medieval medicine. The modern English phrase emerged in the late 1800s as scientific understanding of the enteric nervous system developed. The term gained popularity in the psychological literature of the early 1900s.

Turn a blind eye - To deliberately ignore undesirable information
Origin: This phrase comes from the actions of British Admiral Horatio Nelson at the Battle of Copenhagen in 1801. When signaled to withdraw, Nelson, who had lost sight in one eye in a previous battle, held his telescope to his blind eye and claimed he couldn't see the signal flag. The incident was documented in multiple naval records and biographies and became a popular metaphor for willful ignorance.

Take a turn for the worse - To suddenly deteriorate in health or condition
Origin: This expression emerged from 18th-century medical journals, where physicians noted the "turn" or crisis point in a patient's fever cycle. In the 1670s, Thomas Sydenham, known as the "English Hippocrates," popularized the term through his detailed patient observations. His influential writings described how patients would either "turn" toward recovery or "turn for the worse" at critical junctures in their illness.

Keep a stiff upper lip - To maintain composure in difficult situations
Origin: This phrase emerged from British military culture in the late 1700s, where showing emotion with trembling lips was considered a sign of weakness. The earliest documented use appears in naval officer diaries from the Napoleonic Wars (1803-1815). The phrase became emblematic of British stoicism during the Victorian era and was particularly promoted in boys' public schools.

Survival of the fittest - The continuation of organisms best adapted to their environment
Origin: Herbert Spencer coined this phrase in his 1864 work Principles of Biology after reading Charles Darwin's On the Origin of Species. Darwin adopted the phrase in the 5th edition of Origin (1869), preferring it to his own term, "natural selection." Spencer's phrase quickly entered both scientific discourse and popular culture, though its meaning has often been misinterpreted from its original context.

Lend an ear - To listen attentively or give someone your attention
Origin: This phrase traces back to Shakespeare's "Julius Caesar" (1599), where Mark Antony begins his famous speech with "Friends, Romans, countrymen, lend me your ears." However, the concept dates even further to Medieval times when town criers would request attention by asking people to "lend their ears." The phrase reflects the historical view of attention as a commodity that could be borrowed.

Stick your neck out - To take a risk or make oneself vulnerable
Origin: This phrase originated from medieval execution practices where prisoners would have to extend their necks for

the executioner's axe. The first metaphorical use appears in French court documents from the 1600s. The modern meaning evolved during the American Revolutionary period, where it described taking political risks.

Go under the knife - To undergo surgery
Origin: This phrase dates to the early 1800s, when surgery was performed without anesthesia, with a simple knife as the surgeon's primary tool. The term gained widespread use after Scottish surgeon James Syme documented his surgical techniques using it in 1823. The introduction of ether anesthesia in 1846 made surgery less traumatic, but the dramatic phrase persisted in popular usage.

On the mend - Recovering from illness or injury
Origin: This idiom derives from Middle English medical terminology of the 1400s, where "mend" was used as a technical term for the healing of bones and wounds. The phrase appears in John Arderne's medical treatises from 1376, where he describes patients being "on ye mende" after successful treatments. The term evolved from the Old French "amender," meaning to correct or improve.

Black and blue - Bruised or injured
Origin: The expression originates from Old English medical texts dating to the 9th century, where "blāc and blāw" described the progression of bruise colors. The phrase appears in the Anglo-Saxon Leechbook of Bald, a medical text from around 900 CE that describes trauma treatments. Medieval physicians used these color changes to gauge healing progress, as documented in various medical manuscripts.

Get something off one's chest - To confess or discuss something that has been causing worry

Origin: This phrase emerged from 19th-century tuberculosis treatment practices. Physicians encouraged patients to cough and "get it off their chest" to clear their lungs of fluid. The term first appeared in medical journals around 1820, describing the physical relief patients felt after expectoration. By 1830, it had evolved to encompass emotional relief as well.

Cold shoulder - To treat someone with deliberate coldness or disregard
Origin: This phrase originated in medieval English hospitality customs of the 1300s. When visitors overstayed their welcome, they were served cold shoulder of mutton instead of hot fresh meat. The practice is first documented in the household records of several noble families from the 14th century. Sir Walter Scott popularized the phrase in his 1816 novel The Antiquary, though he was describing an already well-established social custom.

In stitches - Laughing very hard
Origin: This expression derives from medieval medical practices when severe laughter was thought to cause physical pain requiring stitches. The term appears in English medical texts from the 1500s, describing patients laughing so hard they developed side stitches. By the late 17th century, the phrase evolved from a literal medical condition to its figurative meaning.

Out cold - Unconscious or in a deep sleep
Origin: This phrase emerged from 18th-century boxing terminology, specifically from the practice of reviving knocked-out fighters with cold water. The term first appeared in Pierce Egan's "Boxiana" (1812), a comprehensive study of

boxing history. Medical journals of the period began adopting the term to describe various states of unconsciousness, leading to its broader usage.

Rub salt in the wound - To make a difficult situation even worse

Origin: This phrase reflects the ancient medical practice of rubbing salt into wounds as a disinfectant, documented in Egyptian medical papyri from 2500 BCE. Greek physician Hippocrates recommended salt for sterilizing wounds in 400 BCE, and Roman soldiers were issued salt rations partly for this purpose. Though extremely painful, the practice continued through medieval times until more modern antiseptics were developed.

Sleep tight - To sleep soundly and peacefully.

Origin: This phrase dates back to the 18th and 19th centuries when beds were often made with a lattice of ropes that needed to be pulled tight for proper support. A well-tightened bed provided a more comfortable sleep, leading to the phrase "sleep tight." The phrase became widely popular in the 19th century, appearing in literature and bedtime expressions, often accompanied by "don't let the bedbugs bite."

Throw the book at someone - To charge someone with or punish them for every possible infraction
Origin: This phrase originated in American courtrooms in the 1880s, when law books were physically present, and judges would often consult them during proceedings. The earliest documented use appears in the Chicago Tribune, which reported on a judge who "threw the whole law book" at a repeat offender in 1892. The phrase became widespread during the 1930s gangster era.

The long arm of the law - The far-reaching power of legal authorities
Origin: This phrase emerged in the 1800s with the establishment of professional police forces. It first appeared in print in The Times of London in 1823, referring to the newly formed London Metropolitan Police. The phrase gained popularity as telegraph communications allowed law enforcement to coordinate across greater distances, making it harder for criminals to escape justice.

Caught red-handed - To be caught in the act of committing a crime

Origin: This phrase originated in 15th-century Scottish law. The term "red hand" or "bloody hand" was used in medieval Scottish laws to describe someone caught with clear evidence of having committed a crime, particularly theft or murder. The earliest written record appears in the Scottish Acts of Parliament of 1432. Originally specific to cases where a perpetrator was literally caught with blood on their hands from poaching or murder, it gradually expanded to encompass any situation where someone was caught in the act of wrongdoing.

Above the law - Exempt from or not bound by the laws that govern others

Origin: This concept dates back to medieval European monarchies of the 12th and 13th centuries when kings claimed the divine right to rule. The Latin phrase "Rex est lex animate" (the king is the living law) embodied this principle. The modern English phrase gained prominence during the 17th-century English Civil War debates over monarchical power, particularly in parliamentary speeches challenging King Charles I's claim to absolute authority.

Lay down the law - To state rules or commands firmly and explicitly

Origin: This phrase originated in early American frontier towns of the 1820s. As new settlements were established, appointed judges would literally lay down written copies of the law for the community. The first printed use appears in a Missouri gazette from 1826. The phrase quickly evolved into metaphorical use for any authoritative pronouncement.

Get away with murder - To escape punishment for serious wrongdoing

Origin: This idiom emerged from American newspaper coverage in the early 1900s. It first appeared regularly in crime reporting during the 1920s Prohibition era, when gangsters like Al Capone frequently evaded conviction despite widespread knowledge of their crimes. The phrase gained particular prominence during the 1921 trial of Roscoe "Fatty" Arbuckle, where newspapers used it to criticize the justice system. By the 1930s, it had broadened to describe any situation where someone avoided consequences for their actions.

Turn the tables - To reverse a situation, especially to gain the upper hand

Origin: This phrase comes from board games, specifically backgammon, in the 1630s. Players would literally turn the board around to switch positions. The first printed use appears in Francis Bacon's "Of Revenge" (1634), where he uses it metaphorically. The phrase became widely used beyond gaming contexts by the late 1700s.

Take the stand - To testify in court

Origin: This phrase emerged from British courtroom architecture in the 1700s. Prior to this, witnesses testified from the well of the court, but elevated witness boxes or "stands" were introduced for better visibility and acoustics. The first documented use appears in Old Bailey Court records from 1748, and the phrase became standard legal terminology by 1800.

Behind bars - In prison or jail

Origin: The phrase stems from the medieval European prison system of the 1500s. Early jails used actual iron bars in windows and cells, a practice that became standardized during the Tudor period in England. The term appears in prison records and architectural specifications from the reign of Henry VIII. The first literary use was in a 1530 poem describing the Tower of London.

Serve time - To spend time in prison as punishment
Origin: This phrase emerged from the American penal system in the 1860s. It reflects the concept that prison sentences were a debt to society that had to be "served" like a term of service. The phrase first appeared in prison records from New York's Sing Sing Prison in 1865. It became widely used in newspaper crime reporting during the post-Civil War era.

Under lock and key - Securely locked away or stored
Origin: This phrase emerged from medieval English security practices in the 1300s. Early locks required both a physical lock mechanism and a separate key, making items secured this way doubly protected. The phrase appears in household inventories and wills from the 14th century, particularly in reference to valuable items. The earliest written record is found in Chaucer's "Canterbury Tales" (circa 1390).

Law of the land - The established law of a country or region
Origin: This phrase comes from the Latin "lex terrae" in the Magna Carta of 1215. This crucial document, signed by King John of England, established that even monarchs were subject to the law. The English translation "law of the land" first appeared in the Provisions of Oxford in 1258. The concept became a cornerstone of English common law and later American constitutional law.

Legal loophole - An ambiguity or omission in the law that allows one to avoid its intention

Origin: The term originates from arrow slits or "loopholes" in medieval castle walls—narrow openings that allowed defenders to shoot while staying protected. By the 1600s, the term was applied metaphorically to legal documents in England's Court of Chancery. The first recorded legal usage appeared in 1614 in Sir Edward Coke's legal commentaries.

Jury-rigged - Something improvised or assembled quickly with available materials
Origin: This nautical term originated in the mid-18th century during the Age of Sail. When a ship's mast was damaged in battle or storms, sailors would create a temporary replacement called a "jury mast" using whatever materials were available. The term "jury" likely comes from the Old French "ajurie," meaning "aid" or "help." By 1788, the term appeared in maritime dictionaries and gradually expanded beyond nautical use to describe any makeshift repair.

Throw someone under the bus - To betray or sacrifice someone for one's own gain or self-preservation
Origin: This phrase emerged from the world of show business in the 1980s. First documented in a 1982 article in the Washington Post about music promoters, it likely stems from tour buses being a central part of musicians' lives. The specific origin is credited to sports reporter Cyndi Lauperti, who used it extensively in her coverage of the Boston Celtics basketball team. By the 1990s, it had become widely used in political contexts.

Cornered - To be in a difficult situation with no escape
Origin: This term dates back to medieval hunting practices in 14th-century England. During organized hunts, prey animals were deliberately driven into corners of fields or wooded areas

where they could be more easily captured. The term first appeared in Geoffrey Chaucer's The Parliament of Fowls (1382), where he describes a fox being "cornered" by hunting dogs. The metaphorical use evolved during the Tudor period.

Call to the bar - To qualify as a barrister or lawyer
Origin: This phrase originated in the 1300s from the physical layout of English courts. A wooden bar separated the public gallery from the area where judges and lawyers operated. Only qualified lawyers were permitted to stand on the judicial side of this bar to argue cases. The first formal "call to the bar" ceremony was recorded at London's Inns of Court in 1547, establishing a tradition that continues in many Commonwealth countries today.

Scot-free - To escape punishment or consequences completely
Origin: Contrary to popular belief, this phrase has nothing to do with Scottish people. It derives from the Old Norse word "skat," meaning tax or payment, which became "scot" in medieval English. In 13th-century England, a "scot" was a municipal tax, and someone who avoided paying it was said to get away "scot-free." The term appears in numerous medieval tax records and gained its broader meaning by the 16th century.

Above board - Honest, open, and legitimate
Origin: This phrase comes from gambling practices in the 16th century. Card players were required to keep their hands "above board" (visible on the tabletop) to prevent cheating by dealing from below the table. The first documented use appears in Shakespeare's "The Winter's Tale" (1611). During the Elizabethan era, gambling houses began enforcing this

rule strictly, leading to the phrase's adoption in general business contexts.

Behind closed doors - In secret or private, away from public view

Origin: This phrase emerged from medieval European court protocols in the 15th century. Important state decisions were made in the "private chambers" of castles and palaces, where physical doors were indeed closed for secrecy. The term gained prominence during the Congress of Vienna (1814-1815), where major diplomatic decisions were made in private meetings. The phrase became widely used in political journalism by the 1850s.

Below the belt - Unfair or unethical behavior, especially in arguments or competitions.

Origin: This phrase originates from boxing, where hitting an opponent below the beltline is considered an illegal and unsportsmanlike move. The term was formalized in the Marquess of Queensberry Rules, which were established in 1867 to regulate the sport. By the late 19th century, "below the belt" had entered common language as a metaphor for any underhanded or unfair action.

Bail out - To escape from a difficult situation or to provide financial assistance.

Origin: This phrase has two primary origins. In aviation, "bail out" was first used during World War II to describe pilots ejecting from damaged aircraft to save themselves. The financial sense of "bailing out" comes from the legal system, where a person accused of a crime could be released from jail by paying bail money. By the mid-20th century, the term was widely used to describe financial rescues, particularly of companies or economies in crisis.

At loggerheads - In a state of strong disagreement or conflict. **Origin:** The phrase dates back to the 17th century and originally referred to "loggerheads," which were heavy iron tools or clubs used in disputes or fights. The term first appeared in English literature in the 1670s to describe people engaged in serious quarrels. Over time, "at loggerheads" became a widely used idiom for individuals or groups locked in heated arguments or disputes.

Keep your powder dry - Stay prepared for future challenges
Origin: This phrase is attributed to Oliver Cromwell during the Irish Campaign of 1649 when he reportedly told his troops to "trust in God and keep your powder dry." The importance of keeping gunpowder dry was critical in early firearm warfare. The phrase appeared in military manuals throughout the 1600s and became a popular metaphor by the 1800s.

Bite the bullet - To endure a painful or unpleasant situation with fortitude
Origin: This phrase originated from military field medicine in the 1800s. Before the advent of effective anesthetics during the American Civil War (1861-1865), wounded soldiers were given a lead bullet to bite on during emergency surgery. The practice is documented in military medical manuals from the period, including the 1863 U.S. Army Medical Manual. Frederick Marryat's 1891 novel "Children of the New Forest" contains one of the earliest literary uses.

Loose cannon - A dangerously uncontrolled person or thing
Origin: In the age of sailing ships (1700s-1800s), a cannon that broke loose from its mounting during storms or battle could cause devastating damage as it rolled around the deck. Naval officer William Glascock's "Naval Service" (1826) records several incidents of loose cannons causing shipboard catastrophes, and the term became metaphorical by the 1890s.

Call the shots - To be in charge or make decisions
Origin: This phrase originated from billiards/pool in the late 1800s. Players were required to "call their shots" (declare which ball would go into which pocket) before taking them. The first documented non-sporting use appears in the early 1900s in business contexts. By the 1950s, it had become common in political and management terminology.

Meet your Waterloo - To face a final, decisive defeat
Origin: This idiom stems directly from Napoleon Bonaparte's historic defeat at the Battle of Waterloo on June 18, 1815. The battle marked the end of Napoleon's rule as Emperor of the French and concluded his Hundred Days return from exile. The phrase gained popularity in English vernacular during the 1820s as a metaphor for any decisive or crushing defeat. Thomas Hardy's use of it in 1874's "Far from the Madding Crowd" helped cement its place in common usage.

On the warpath - In an angry, aggressive mood, ready for conflict
Origin: This phrase comes from Native American warfare practices, specifically the path warriors took when heading to battle. Early American colonial documents from the 1750s describe these war trails. The term gained widespread use during the American frontier expansion of the 1800s and

frequently appeared in newspaper coverage of conflicts between settlers and Native Americans.

Take no prisoners - To act with maximum aggression or total commitment

Origin: This phrase stems from actual military orders, particularly during medieval and early modern warfare when capturing and ransoming prisoners was common practice. The command to "take no prisoners" meant showing no mercy and killing all enemy combatants. The practice was formally documented in military records during the Thirty Years' War (1618-1648). The metaphorical usage emerged in business contexts during the late Victorian era.

Give no quarter - Show no mercy; refuse to spare an opponent

Origin: The term originated in naval and land warfare of the 16th and 17th centuries. "Quarter" referred to the promise of shelter or safe housing for surrendering enemies. The phrase appears in Spanish Armada documents from 1588 and became common in English naval records during the Anglo-Dutch Wars (1652-1674). Shakespeare used a variation of the phrase in "Henry IV, Part 1" (1597).

In the trenches - Engaged in hard, continuous work or warfare

Origin: This phrase comes directly from the trench warfare experience of World War I (1914-1918). British and French military records detail the harsh conditions of trench life, where soldiers spent weeks in muddy, dangerous conditions. War correspondents' reports from 1915-1917 helped spread understanding of trench warfare conditions. The metaphorical usage became common in business contexts during the 1920s.

Zero hour - The crucial moment when something important is to begin

Origin: This military term emerged during World War I, first documented in 1914 military communications. It referred to the exact time an attack or military operation was to begin, traditionally written as "H-hour." The term gained civilian usage after the war, particularly in project management and deadline contexts.

Hold your ground - To maintain one's position and not retreat, either literally or figuratively

Origin: This military phrase dates back to the 14th century, during the rise of infantry warfare in medieval Europe. It first appeared in written form in English military documents around 1380, specifically in training manuals for longbow archers. The phrase gained prominence during the Hundred Years' War (1337-1453) where English commanders would order their troops to "hold their ground" against French cavalry charges. By the 16th century, the phrase had evolved beyond military usage into general parlance.

Fight fire with fire - To respond to an attack by using the same methods as your opponent

Origin: This phrase originated in the American frontier during the early 1800s from the practice of setting controlled backfires to stop advancing wildfires. When faced with an approaching prairie fire, settlers would deliberately burn a strip of land ahead of the wildfire, creating a barrier of consumed fuel. The earliest documented use appears in an 1837 issue of the "Maine Farmer" newspaper, describing frontier firefighting techniques. By the 1850s, the phrase had become metaphorical.

Bring out the big guns - To use one's most powerful or forceful means of attack or persuasion

Origin: The phrase emerged from naval warfare in the late 18th century, when ships initially engaged with smaller weapons before revealing their largest cannons. The term "big guns" specifically referred to the heavy cannons introduced on British Royal Navy ships during the Napoleonic Wars (1803-1815). The first recorded metaphorical use appears in British naval officer James Hardy Vaux's 1819 memoir, where he describes diplomatic negotiations using this military metaphor. By the 1850s, the phrase had entered common usage in both Britain and America.

Over the top - To go beyond normal limits or expectations; to be excessive

Origin: This phrase originated in World War I, specifically referring to soldiers climbing out of their trenches to attack enemy positions. The term first appeared in British military documents around 1916, describing the deadly practice of scaling trench walls to charge across "no man's land." Field Marshal Sir Douglas Haig's orders for the Battle of the Somme in 1916 repeatedly used this phrase, which became symbolic of the war's devastating human cost. By the 1920s, the term had entered civilian speech, shifting from its literal military meaning to describe any excessive action.

Flash in the pan - Something that shows initial promise but fails to deliver lasting success

Origin: The phrase comes from the flintlock musket mechanism of the 1630s. The pan was a small depression that held priming powder. When struck, it would create a flash but sometimes fail to ignite the main charge in the barrel. This common misfire was first documented in military training manuals from the English Civil War (1642-1651). The term became widespread in military reports during the American Revolution, with George Washington notably complaining about "flash-in-the-pan" recruits in his correspondence of 1777.

Run the gauntlet - To endure a series of difficulties, challenges, or criticisms
Origin: This punishment ritual originated in 16th-century Germanic and Swedish armies (where it was called "gatlop"). Offending soldiers were forced to run between two rows of fellow soldiers who would strike them with rods or rope ends. The practice was officially documented in the Swedish military law of 1546 under King Gustav I. The term entered the English vernacular through Scottish mercenaries serving in Swedish armies during the Thirty Years' War (1618-1648). By the late 1700s, it had evolved into a metaphor for facing any series of ordeals.

Draw a bead - To take careful aim at something; to focus attention on a target
Origin: This phrase emerged from early 19th-century American frontier rifle terminology. The "bead" referred to the small metal ball at the end of a rifle barrel, used for precise aiming. The term first appeared in print in James Fenimore Cooper's "The Last of the Mohicans" (1826), describing marksmen's techniques during the French and Indian War. The phrase gained popularity during the American Civil War when rifle technology and marksmanship became increasingly sophisticated.

Caught in the crossfire - To be caught between two opposing forces or arguments

Origin: The term originated in military tactics of the 18th century, specifically during the American Revolution. It described the deadly situation of being trapped between two lines of fire in a military maneuver called "cross firing," first documented in British Army field manuals of 1776. General Washington's papers from Valley Forge (1777-1778) contain multiple references to using crossfire tactics against British formations. The metaphorical usage emerged during the Civil War period as newspaper reporters began using it to describe political conflicts.

Pass muster - To meet required standards; to be acceptable
Origin: This phrase dates back to 16th-century military inspections. The term "muster" comes from Medieval Latin "monstrare" (to show), and referred to the formal process of gathering troops for inspection and counting. King Henry VIII's military reforms of 1515 established regular muster requirements for English troops, with detailed records kept in "muster books." The phrase first appeared in Shakespeare's "Henry IV, Part 2" (1599) and maintained its military meaning until the 19th century, when it broadened into civilian use.

Rank and file - Ordinary members of an organization or group rather than its leaders
Origin: The term comes from military formation organization dating to the Spanish tercio system of the 1530s. "Rank" referred to soldiers standing shoulder-to-shoulder in a horizontal line, while "file" meant a vertical column of soldiers. The phrase appears in English military documents from the reign of Elizabeth I, particularly in training manuals from 1578. The term became especially prominent during the English Civil War (1642-1651) when Parliament's New Model Army established standardized drilling procedures.

Armed to the teeth - Heavily armed or well-prepared for a confrontation.

Origin: This phrase originates from 17th-century piracy, particularly among Caribbean buccaneers. Pirates and soldiers were often described as being "armed to the teeth," meaning they carried weapons in every possible way, including knives, swords, pistols, and even extra daggers in their mouths. The phrase was first recorded in English literature in the late 1600s and later became a general term for being heavily equipped or prepared.

Dead in the water - Completely stuck or unable to progress.

Origin: This phrase comes from maritime terminology and refers to a ship that has lost all momentum, often due to a lack of wind or a failed engine. It has been used in nautical contexts since at least the 18th century. By the 20th century, "dead in the water" had evolved into a metaphorical phrase describing anything that had stalled or failed to move forward.

Red herring - A misleading clue or distraction.

Origin: The term "red herring" dates back to 18th-century England and was associated with the practice of using strong-smelling smoked fish to distract hunting dogs from their intended scent trail. The phrase was later used figuratively by writers and debaters to describe misleading arguments or diversions. It gained prominence in detective fiction and journalism by the 19th and 20th centuries as a term for false leads or deceptive tactics.

TURN THE PAGE FOR A FREE BONUS BOOK!

http://geni.us/IdiomsReview

CONCLUSION

Well, look at you—going the whole nine yards and making it to the finish line! Hopefully, along the way, you've had a few aha! moments, maybe even dropped some knowledge on unsuspecting friends or impressed someone at a dinner party with your newfound idiom expertise. (You're welcome.)

Language is weird, wonderful, and ever-changing, and idioms are proof of that. Who would've thought that spilled beans could mean more than just a mess on the floor? Or that buttering someone up had such sticky, ancient origins? And let's be honest, now that you know where kicking the bucket really came from, you may never hear it the same way again.

But before you ride off into the sunset, I have a small favor to ask. **If you enjoyed this book, I'd love it if you could leave a quick review on Amazon.**

https://geni.us/IdiomsReview

Just a sentence or two is enough to help fellow language lovers decide if this is their cup of tea (see what I did there?).

And because I appreciate you sticking it out to the very end, I've got a little something extra for you—a **free bonus book** as a thank-you! Just head to **https://geni.us/SayWhatBonus**, and I'll send it straight to your inbox.

Now, go forth and sprinkle these idioms into your conversations! You never know when someone might ask, "Say what?", and you can finally have all the answers. Happy reading, and keep those words flowing!

CLAIM YOUR FREE GIFT!

Scan the QR code below to
download your free bonus gift!

Or go to
http://geni.us/SayWhatBonus

www.ingramcontent.com/pod-product-compliance
Lightning Source LLC
Chambersburg PA
CBHW071517120626
46550CB00006B/2253